THE
EDUCATED
GUESS

How to challenge invisible
biases and make better
education choices

WARWICK
SHARP

Creative works and print by Spiffing Covers

CONTENTS

INTRODUCTION

Education opens the door to the future. It allows us to go wherever our hard work and talents can take us. People who have had a good education can enjoy their full share of citizenship, shape the world around them, and enrich their own lives and the lives of others.

But it all depends on the choices we make. Take the big decisions, such as choosing schools or picking options for qualifications. These decisions are a big responsibility, with far-reaching consequences, and we need to get them right.

Let's be clear, we often do get them right; and alongside all the available advice, information and evidence out there, our personal judgement is the most powerful tool we have in making these life-shaping decisions. After all, a parent knows their child better than anyone else possibly could, in the same way that a teacher's understanding of their class is unrivalled.

But, at the same time, our choices can sometimes be based on thinking biases, which can distort our decisions more than we might realise. Decades' worth of research and evidence backs this up.

But, to prove the point, let's glance back at the history of education in our country and what people once believed – and, in some cases, not so very long ago.

Britain – the first industrialised country – was the last major European country to have a free universal education system.[1] It was believed for a long time that education should be managed through voluntary contributions; arguments against educating everyone included concerns that if the poor could read they would be influenced by rebellious pamphlets and be led astray.[2] Another example is the official report in 1923, which reflected the widely held view that boys had a habit of 'healthy idleness', whereas girls could be trusted to use free time well and, in fact, needed it more because they were less able to protect themselves from pressure.[3]

The story of education in the UK is peppered with similar examples of how what we thought was right at the time shaped decisions that were made, and greatly affected people's lives. What these points in history have in common is that we were initially convinced that one approach was right, and then suddenly we weren't.

Fast-forwarding to the present day, how could we claim even now, as enlightened as we think we are, that we always get it right? In medicine, we can't claim to have reached the zenith of our knowledge; in technology, there is no sign that we will ever stop innovating; and when it comes to the environment, what was once acceptable is now being rewritten.

The simple truth is, we are human and we can't assume we're going to get it all right. But what we can do is look at a wide base of evidence and advice, and that includes the thinking biases that affect us all even though they are invisible to us.

The Educated Guess is designed to be a thought-provoking discussion of some of those biases, specifically in relation to education, but these are also relevant to many other parts of our lives. It provides directly applicable examples of some of the biggest tricks our minds play on us when it comes to education, and empowers us to make more informed, beneficial choices.

We will start by examining how these choices can be based more on thinking biases than we realise, and how relying on intuition alone can sometimes lead us down the wrong path. Each is discussed in a short, sharp chapter intended to stimulate our thinking and challenge what we currently believe.

This is a practical book for people who lead busy lives but who are open to advice. It is a book for those interested in the flaws in our intuition, and when we need to think in a broader or deeper way.

Spanning education in its widest sense, and taking into consideration the areas where challenging thinking biases offers the greatest potential for improving our choices, *The Educated Guess* is structured into three parts, as follows.

Part 1: *The Bigger Picture will discuss:*

- How media coverage can present the world as a more negative and dangerous place than it actually is, thus affecting our decisions.

- Why focussing too heavily on single pieces of information, such as class size, when making decisions can distort our choices.

- Why we might be prone to downgrade certain areas of education that are harder to measure, such as character education, despite compelling evidence to the contrary.

*In Part 2: **Our Own Path** we will look at:*

- Why we rely on the experiences of people around us to shape our decisions, particularly to do with vocational education, even though they are not always the best guide for determining our own path.

- Why we are influenced by extreme success stories when deciding our personal career aspirations, despite them not being representative of what most journeys are actually like.

- Why we become overly attached to the status quo, thus slowing our ability to adjust to changing circumstances and skills needs.

*In Part 3: **The Wider World** we will discuss a different kind of thinking bias at play when decisions we make at an individual level may intuitively make sense, but how the impact on the wider world is worth considering. Specifically:*

- Why we are drawn to people "like us" when making choices about education institutions, but how that can lead to more segregation and less social cohesion.

- Why we are less likely to intervene and help when there are other people around, the end result often being that no one steps in until it's too late, even in serious cases of bullying or child abuse.

Intuition and Thinking Biases

Before we dive in, some opening context is important. The world is a complex place and we don't have the capacity, or frankly enough time or patience, to analyse every piece of evidence when making decisions. Therefore, we often take shortcuts, or rush, rather than sit down to examine all the possible arguments. So, let us briefly look at how thinking biases and intuition are at play.

Intuition in this context is when we think we know something without needing to go through the evidence, proof or reasoning; it is the result of how our brains store, process and recall information on a subconscious level. Intuitions are more than just hunches; they can seem so certain, and they profoundly shape our attitudes, views and thoughts.

There is compelling evidence that we all make decisions based on intuition much more than we might think, and the intuitive part of our mind is far more powerful than most people realise.[4] This research has changed how we think about the human mind.[5] We have the deliberate and logical part of our brain, which is excellent at analysing and making decisions, but which requires a lot of energy. And then there is the other part of our brain, which is intuitive, fast and automatic.

Research shows that the intuitive part of our brains plays an important role, as much of what we absorb unconsciously is highly relevant, and sometimes invaluable. Indeed, it can even be lifesaving. For example, when walking down a dark alleyway it is intuition which can help us "sense" a mugger in time to run away, when pausing to analyse all the available information would put us at risk. And when we're driving down the motorway, it is intuition that often spots a dangerous driver long before we've observed enough of their behaviour to know this through normal rational thinking.

But intuition can be wrong, too. Why? Because although a thing might "feel" right or wrong, *it doesn't mean that it is*. Intuition, whilst fast and automatic, is riddled with what we call "cognitive biases". Dozens have been identified, and they affect everything we do.[6] And despite these biases, our intuition doesn't wait for the logical, analytical part of our brain to catch up before offering up its assessment of a situation or issue. All the time it is picking up bits of information and matching them with something similar in our database of memories, and combining them to arrive at a conclusion. In practice, that is how we make many of our decisions.

The book discusses thinking biases at work, how they play out in the moment, the benefit of considering evidence to the contrary, and an alternative way forward, thus encouraging deeper thought and reflection.

Ultimately, decisions will always remain up to us, but we are only really free to make the best choices if we are empowered to see through some of the main thinking biases, understand how intuition can work both for and against, and how broader and deeper thinking will bring us to the best choices.

Decision-making and Education

These thinking biases can have substantial real-world impact, and the impact is perhaps even greater when it comes to education, because it is such a critical part of our lives, with a large volume of detail to try and process. And because every single person has some experience of it, education is also especially vulnerable to the fact that we can believe we understand how something works even when our understanding might be superficial.[7] For instance, in an experiment focused on asking a group of people if they know how a fridge works, many say yes; but when tested they realise that they don't actually know much at all, beyond some basic information. In other words, we can mistake basic familiarity with understanding.

This is cause enough for any of us to pause and reflect on our decisions about education, because whether our choices affect ourselves, our children or others, getting it right matters a great deal.

Let's not overreact, though. Many of our intuitions about education are useful, and even when they are not, some do not lead to decisions of major significance. Choosing history or geography GCSE doesn't tend to irrevocably change most people's life chances; and some decisions we've made that later feel wrong can be corrected. For example, if we didn't initially sign a child up for an extra-curricular activity that may benefit their development, we can always change our mind at a later date.

Neither should we under-react, especially given the significant amount of freedom we have to make education choices. The impact in some cases can be substantial, far-reaching and long lasting.

We can also consider the knock-on effects of our decisions. Decisions we make are replicated many times – potentially over 10 million times for all of the children in the country at the moment – and they determine what education looks like in our country. We all influence the education system directly, as it is made up of all of us and what we do. For instance, if more of us pay attention to published data about academic performance, that increasingly becomes the way in which education institutions compete; and if more of us worry about child safety, schools will put more focus on safeguarding children and implement further measures to do this effectively. In this respect, our decisions are most definitely amplified.

But the aim of this book is not to cover every possible avenue and implication of education. To do so would be impractical. Instead, this book prompts us to reflect on what our intuition and thinking biases are telling us in connection to eight key areas. Each is explored in its own chapter, including through real-life examples drawn from wide-ranging research and discussion which represent arguably the most prominent issues with our current thinking. The solutions are in our hands much more than we might realise.

So, let us begin.

Part One

THE BIGGER PICTURE

Chapter One

PROTECTIVE INSTINCTS

Risk-taking fascinates us, and it always has. To cite an example, tightrope walking can be traced all the way back to ancient Greece, and there was even some debate about whether it should feature in the Olympic Games.[8] When, in 1974, Philippe Petit walked between the World Trade Centre's Twin Towers, he was a quarter of a mile above the ground.[9] In 2012, Nik Wallenda walked directly over Niagara Falls – and across the widest point of the river just to make it more dangerous![10]

Other extreme stunts – or risks, depending on our point of view – include climbing Mount Everest in nothing but shorts, diving over 200m in one single breath, jumping across the Grand Canyon on a motorbike, and freefalling from a height of 26 miles to Earth. Few readers of this book are about to try anything like that, I'm sure, and the author certainly will not; but we can all appreciate that risk-taking plays an important role in life, and while feats like these are not necessary and we could do without them, many of our greatest achievements wouldn't happen without at least some element of risk.

Examples of risk-taking of this kind could include Orville and Wilbur Wright flying their aircraft, not knowing for sure whether it would crash into the ground like other attempts before them.[11] Francis Drake could have given up on circumnavigating the world when four of his five ships were destroyed.[12] But these people did take risks, and changed our known world beyond recognition.

In our own adult lives, we know that sometimes, when we put one foot in front of the other, we don't know exactly where we are going, and there will be experimentation along the way. But when it comes to children and young people, what is our view of risk? How comfortable are we exposing them to it?

NEGATIVE NEWS

In order to make decisions about risk, we need to try and understand the real threats that are out there. Few of us have time to dive into detailed national statistics, or try and unpick the latest patterns in any depth, so an obvious source of information about risk – whether or not we are actively seeking it out – is the media.

There are two big problems with that approach though. First, news is always about things that happen, not things that don't happen. ("War Has Not Broken Out" or "No Children Were Bullied This Morning" are not headlines you are ever likely to see.) Second, when we look at the things that do happen, negative stories get more and more attention,[13] often providing a blow-by-blow commentary that seems to rely on some kind of shock factor. By contrast, good news tends to unfold more slowly. For instance, a drop in car burglaries in a certain area happens at too slow a pace to be in sync with the right here, right now news cycle, and in that respect may never reach us.

We are susceptible to the distortions this creates in the media because of something called the "availability bias": we estimate the probability of an event occurring based on how easily examples come to mind.[14] In many ways this is an entirely sensible way of navigating life, as thinking back to when you cut it too tight timewise and missed your last train, for example, makes it less likely that you will make that mistake again.

Another aspect of distortion is the fact that news items can stick in our minds, not because of probability or likelihood, but because they are upsetting or gory or vivid. As a result, we can mis-calibrate risk, and this can play out in a number of ways. For instance, studies show that we are intuitively afraid of shark attacks not because of the likelihood of them happening, but rather because of the nature of an attack and how gruesome it would be.[15]

This bias in our thinking affects almost every aspect of life and people from all walks of life. Investors will often make judgements about stocks and shares based on what they've heard about them in the news (and perhaps find they then underperform).[16] Doctors who have spotted cases of serious disease are more likely to diagnose the next patient with the same disease, even if symptoms are much milder.[17] Indeed, whole commercial strategies rely on the fact that we think in this way. As a converse example, when lottery companies share the exceptional stories of recent winners, they know we will think we are more likely to win ourselves and forget about the miniscule probability of actually doing so![18]

So when it comes to children and young people, these thinking biases can make us more anxious and worried about every aspect of their upbringing. We see news coverage of an abduction or terrible accident in a school, for example, and can forget that these are extremely rare occurrences which generate strong emotional responses rather than a more representative picture of the norm. And the more we think about this kind of tragic event, the more we overestimate the chance of something similar happening to us. As a consequence, we end up thinking the world is a more dangerous place for children and young people than it actually is, and that they are at risk unless they are under close supervision, all the time. So how does this view of risk manifest?

RISK AVERSION

Some recent trends suggest that this constant stream of reported threats and dangers, combined with other factors, such as our natural protective instincts, mean that we are becoming more risk averse. Fewer than half of children walk or cycle to school.[19] And there is a big drop in the number of children who walk to school alone in the UK compared with other countries, like Germany, suggesting that such choices are not always an inevitable consequence of modern-day life.[20]

Studies show that children play outside now for an average of only a few hours a week.[21] And research suggests the distance children stray from home on their own is seriously limited by historic standards in terms of type and variety of space visited and activities undertaken (unless directly facilitated by parents).[22]

More generally, parental attitudes towards supervision show a growing consensus that children and young people need an adult with them at all times.[23] Indeed, a poll revealed that almost half of adults questioned thought the earliest age that a child should go out unsupervised was 14.[24]

As well as what is happening outside of formal education, schools respond to the concerns of parents about child safety and supervision – entirely understandably – to the point where the former head of the health and safety executive warned about an "excessive risk-averse" culture in schools.[25] This refers to excessive worries about health and safety, which can often be "nonsensical".

To look at some examples, traditional games like conkers, leapfrog and British Bulldog are banned in some schools.[26] Increasing numbers of children on school trips are made to wear hi-vis jackets – in the words of the Ofsted chief inspector, "like troupes of tiny construction workers – minus the hard hats".[27] The chief inspector has cited other examples, including sports days cancelled for "dew on the grass" and fears about "the dangers of air-filled balloons."[28] The impact reaches other fields, too. For instance, training to be a nanny for privileged families can involve skid pan driving courses, learning about the Internet from former military intelligence officers, and self-defence classes.[29]

In recent years, the Internet has become yet another subject of great concern, where exposure to the digital world, with its outside threats and dangers, is brought right within the home. Research suggests this is a top worry, with nearly three-quarters of parents in one survey believing that the Internet is unsafe for children to explore unsupervised.[30] There has also been a steady decline in the proportion of parents who believe that the benefits of the Internet for children outweigh any risks.[31] Responses range from supervision and monitoring tools, all the way to outright bans.

When taken together and extrapolated over the course of childhood, by age 16, or 18, or even 21 – at which point we have historically entered adulthood – young people today have hit fewer milestones and have less developmental experience than ever before. Landmark research in the United States has found that young people are growing up more slowly than previous generations due to less unsupervised time and less autonomy and independence.[32] There are parallels with the experiences of young people in the UK.[33]

THE REAL WORLD

In reality, the world isn't as dangerous as we might be led to think, and some aspects of modern life are enlightening, including major long-term changes in rates of poverty, murder and democracy, which are all moving in a positive direction.[34]

In many ways, children are safer now than at any point in history, and this is far from as simple as the impact of the trends mentioned earlier. In fact, there have been some big shifts, and positive ones. Simple inventions like childproof medicine caps have cut accidents across the board, not just in our own homes.[35] Children and young people are less likely to be victims of violent crime; and risky behaviours like binge drinking and smoking have substantially declined.[36]

Looking at figures for England – with similar trends across the whole of the UK – child deaths are in long-term decline, with a more than 50% drop in the average rate of child deaths caused by assault since the early 1980s.[37] Child casualties on the road are also down substantially, by more than 80% since 1979.[38]

The more alarming causes of injury and death have a tendency to stick in the mind, even if they are becoming less and less likely. But the fact is, the trend towards a reduction in deaths – in water, for example – continues.[39] Similarly, serious electric shocks actually pose very little risk and are not as common as many people think.[40] By far the most common cause of accident is falling over, and many falls are not classed as preventable accidents given that stumbles and trips happen as part of rapid child development.[41]

Surveys show that the scale of some perceived risks, especially around "stranger danger", do not match either the actual statistics or create any real cause for greater concern.[42] Indeed, there is much more debate these days about whether "stranger danger" is even the right message for children, and there has been a switch to "clever never goes" instead, devised to make children less afraid of the world by giving them the confidence to make decisions about their own personal safety.[43]

Returning to the subject of the Internet, it is becoming clearer that the perceived risks around the digital world are not always backed up by the reality either. For instance, a landmark study found that the claims that screen time can cause depression and serious mental health issues are unfounded.[44] In fact, a decade's worth of data from British teenagers found a "miniscule" and "trivial" impact of screen time.

The point here is that when we home in on what the media presents as absolute fact, we have a tendency to use its leaning towards bad or dramatic news as our main frame of reference, and allow it to colour our decisions. In truth, these are just snapshots of a much bigger picture, and it would serve us well to remember this when making decisions.

NO SUBSTITUTE FOR EXPERIENCE

If the world is as dangerous as it can sometimes

be made out to be, then the temptation is to go for maximum protection. But doing so comes at a cost, and that cost is experience. It is widely understood that children and young people develop in so many ways when they learn from experience – in truth, we all do, and every day – and as a consequence then learn to adapt to their environment. Therefore, some of the experiences currently dismissed as "too risky" may well be worth it, after all.

Research suggests that exposure to risk is also vital for overcoming fear and anxiety, whereas without risk fears can continue, despite no longer being relevant. In infancy, children develop fears of certain stimuli – for example, heights – to protect them against situations they are not mature enough to cope with; but age-appropriate exposure to heights can be an exhilarating experience for a child, creating the positive emotion of overcoming fear rather than the fear becoming more exaggerated.[45]

When it comes to physical activity, we know that children and young people need to take risks and challenge themselves when involved in play, sport and other activities so that they can learn their own boundaries.[46] Indeed, the evidence is clear that fear of risk can paradoxically put children and young people at greater danger in the long run, given the benefits of physical activity as opposed to the consequences of a sedentary lifestyle.[47]

An example might be an after-school sports activity which we don't think they are physically ready for, perhaps rugby. But allowing them to participate can throw up various benefits, from learning to be part of a team to understanding the rules of play and tactics. They may come home with a few bruises, and the disappointment of losing a match; but look at the upsides of the experience: a young person developing interests and, more importantly, growing in skills and confidence.

This raises a point about emotions. Strong emotions like disappointment or regret are counterfactual, which means they involve us thinking about how things might have been if they'd turned out differently, or if we had made a different decision. This provides children and young people with invaluable experience for when they face disappointment in the future,[48] because, let's face it, not everything goes according to plan!

Crucially, experiences can be controlled and managed. This is very different to just letting children and young people do what they want.

For instance, we might make the assumption that children are not capable of getting themselves to school safely at age nine; but walking the route with them a few times might prove that by the time they are nine and a quarter, they are.

Of course we want to protect children, but we can avoid protection becoming overprotection. To help illustrate this point in a slightly different way, evidence shows that peanut allergies have surged *because* parents started protecting children from exposure to peanuts back in the 1990s. This was well intentioned, but ultimately ineffective, as early eating of peanuts generally leads to a *protective* immune response instead of an allergic immune response. Indeed, among children who had been "protected" from peanuts, 17% developed an allergy, while only 3% of those deliberately exposed developed an allergy.[49]

This example is useful for two reasons. First, because it is striking and it counters long-standing advice that young children should avoid allergenic foods such as peanuts in order to prevent allergies developing. Secondly, because it is an example which applies in so many other areas too. The immune system is like many other parts of us: it adapts to our environment – but *only* if it gets the right exposure to learn how to deal with threats.

In terms of exposure to life's experiences, small challenges are safer at first, obviously, and bigger challenges can be introduced along the way. We would never expose children to equipment, for instance, that may harm them. But – depending on age, of course – where is the harm in giving them some basic tools and materials to play about with? They're going to have to learn to use those things one day, anyway, and far more dangerous tools too, so this early exposure will teach them respect for each tool and what it does, as well as improving their motor skills and confidence.

Outside environments can be stimulating, and experiences such as adventure learning have a positive impact on academic learning, as well as providing benefits like improved self-confidence.[50] Risky play can help us better understand the dangers, too.[51] For example, getting into the odd scrape helps children regulate aggression, and actually teaches them the vital life skills of negotiation and compromise, just as getting lost helps us learn to navigate.

There is no substitute for experiencing things directly. It puts us in touch with what we are capable of, and not capable of yet. It is fascinating that when you ask students about their abilities they often overestimate their skills levels – and clearly if most think they are "above average" they can't all be right![52] A rather sombre example of this kind of self-deception is the Holocaust. It is incredible that 5% of adults in the UK do not believe the Holocaust happened, and one in 12 think its scale has been exaggerated.[53] Events like these, whilst traumatic to learn about, provide invaluable lessons on a world scale, not just on a personal level, on how to avoid a similar thing happening in the future. Therefore, exposure to the real world is critical for tackling self-deception on a small and a large scale.

Our final point here has to do with child and adolescent development in a digital age, where interactions online provide opportunities as well as potential risks. The international evidence shows those benefits can be critical, including opening up new learning opportunities, understanding more about civic engagement, and working out how to communicate and connect.[54] As in so many other situations, the tools and advice exist which both make safe use possible and provide access to the opportunities.

LOOKING AHEAD

To be clear, children and young people still need enormous care and protection throughout their lives, therefore risk should only be measured risk, and we need to use our better judgement in gauging what they are capable of. Sometimes that will mean saying no when all they want to hear is yes; but in order to empower young people, and help them prepare for the long run, we can allow them freedom to move when we think they are ready, to conduct their own exploration of the world around them, and hopefully see it as a place of opportunity.

When we make quick judgements about risk it can help to remember that the examples we recall are not representative and in fact tend to be highly unusual. By doing so, we can look beyond single and isolated cases when something terrible happens. Instead, we can keep them in perspective even if they loom large in our memories. We can think about how exposure to the risks of life will help children and young people develop, and how every experience is an opportunity to grow rather than bunker down. In short, all activities have benefits, and these can outweigh the small amount of risk attached to them.

When you look at a young child, he or she is often fearless, and of course we need to protect them and guide them, but not so much that we over-protect them in a way which is disproportionate to the actual risks rather than the perceived risks. Instead, while it may feel a little uncomfortable at first, we can think about what we want for them in the future – namely to be able to confidently and capably navigate the modern world. To do that they need to have a healthy range of experiences so they can learn and adapt. And the world is a safer place for them to have those experiences than we might intuitively think.

Chapter Two

THE NARROW LENS

We have seen a tremendous expansion in knowledge and ideas, and our ability to share them across the world. The invention of writing, to the development of the printing press, to the introduction of the Internet, were all pivotal moments. Consequently, the amount of information available to us all is vast – and growing at an unprecedented rate.

One thing that hasn't developed at the same rate, though, is our physical ability to process all of this information. Our brains cannot realistically cope with all of the data available from all different directions – emails, messages, news updates, podcasts, etc – and if we did try to keep up with it, studies show this would leave us unable to relax and anxious.[55]

It is no wonder that so much attention in everyday life is given to cutting through the noise and distractions around us so we can concentrate on the important things.

Learning to focus helps in lots of ways. If you are trying to balance on one leg – presumably for the purpose of some kind of stretching or sporting activity – focusing on a single point on the ground helps.[56] When we do that our inner ears are more able to sense our movement and give feedback to our bodies, so that we can counteract any shifts which could throw us off balance. That's not to say that we lose sight of the bigger space around us, just that for the purposes of that specific activity we must narrow our focus for a short time. Clearly, if we approached most activities by staring only at a single point on the ground we wouldn't get very far!

When it comes to education, how do we know when to focus in and when to zoom out to see the bigger picture?

FOCUSING EFFECT

A common bias in our thinking is to rely too much on single factors or attributes when making decisions. These become the focus and, once in place, all of our other, broader thinking and analysis can get less attention.[57]

A famous study which provides evidence for this type of thinking bias was when Americans were asked whether Californians or Mid-Westerners led happier lives, and people overwhelmingly assumed it was Californians.[58] They fell victim to thinking bias, or a narrow focus, as they immediately thought about the better weather, conjured images of a relaxed lifestyle, and of living by the sea. In fact, there is no discernible difference between the happiness of the residents in the two areas at all, and actually some important determinants were overlooked, such as safety from natural disasters.

This narrow focusing effect can influence all parts of our lives. When we buy a second-hand car we might get fixated on criteria like the mileage and use it to determine our purchase, thus overlooking all sorts of other factors, such as service history. And doctors are trained to be aware of drawing judgements too early based on certain criteria, which could lead them to particular conclusions independent of further symptoms or observations.

Focusing too narrowly can mean we don't give enough thought to more of the available information and other possible options, because we're basing our thinking on a reference point presented to us early on in our decision-making. In education, we are susceptible to this thinking bias because we are often presented with information ahead of a decision which seems really important. It is easy for this early information to become the thing that determines our future thinking, and it sticks in our minds more than we might realise.

This matters a great deal, because when it comes to education we actually have substantial freedom to decide what is important to us when comparing and choosing between institutions, from schools to nurseries to universities. This is very unlike other parts of our lives, where there is more of a rulebook in place. For instance, if you break your arm, you are prescribed specific treatment and won't have much say over it, and you don't tend to decide for yourself when to take the cast off. And as you drive a car from one place to the other, how you do that is heavily prescribed and it is clear what is and isn't acceptable. For instance, exercising your freedom of choice and deciding to run red lights or drive on the right (when in the UK) is never going to be a good decision!

Decisions about education will never be quite as straightforward. Realistically, it will never be a case of a child automatically going to a particular school, travelling down one fixed path, with a pre-determined destination when they leave formal education. Choice plays an important role. But the amount of information available can seem overwhelming, and we sometimes respond by narrowing in too much on the factors which are drawn to our immediate attention, and other background factors can easily be crowded out.

This fits wider research which shows that we use less information to make decisions than we think.[59] This is true across a wide spectrum of decisions from choosing a drink, to judging artwork, to analysing performance, to managing employees. Instead of considering the broader picture, we make up our minds as we go along, and form judgements based on the points immediately in front of us – and vital information can remain uncovered or overlooked.

This looking for shortcuts applies as much to when we make choices about education as to anything else. To illustrate, arguably one of the most important education decisions is choosing a school, college or university, so that would seem the point at which we would expend the most effort working through the available information and data. But a major survey showed that more than half of people who made school choices did not look at performance table information that showed what children in a certain school were achieving results-wise, for instance, and more than a third did not look at Ofsted reports.[60]

Instead, other factors drove their decisions. As you might expect, location was a particularly important one.[61] But others, surprisingly, got overlooked. For instance, in a major survey fewer than half of parents thought preference of the child was very important, and only 17% of parents paid much attention to the feeder secondary school when choosing a primary school.[62]

As we go through the decision-making process, it is easy to "narrow down" on particular attributes. Class size is a classic example, and is the basis upon which many private schools market themselves. In fact, 90% of people who send their children to private school say it is "very" or "fairly important".[63] Other examples might be hearing from neighbours that the school their children go to has a certain number of teaching assistants, or that a nephew is at an academy sponsored by a company which provides two mentors for each student, who he meets with regularly. Or we might see a college advertised drawing attention to a range of new buildings, with stunning architecture, and home in on this as a deciding factor.

NO MAGIC NUMBERS

In reality, any single piece of information will struggle to bear the weight we can end up putting on it. Single inputs with respect to education can only tell us so much; and no single factor can make as much difference as we might intuitively think.

Let's come back to class size. It is not credible that anyone could defend a statement like, "Research says class size must be X." Yet intuitively it makes sense to many of us that giving teachers fewer students to teach would make a big difference. This, naturally, is a popular idea, and is a key draw of many schools, and a selling point on countless open days across the country.

We can easily form images in our minds of smaller numbers of happy students, with fewer distractions around them, and more equipment and materials to go round. We might envisage students connecting more closely with one another, with more opportunities to participate; teachers more able to observe and assess progress, with more time for feedback and one-to-one support.

Reducing class size is an appealing and visible way to target parents. We are drawn to it because it is an easy idea to process in our minds, and so we are more likely to believe it is beneficial. It is also framed in a positive way to us, and those who made education decisions on the basis of small class sizes are biased towards defending them in order to justify their decisions to themselves and others.

But things are not always as they seem. Could it be that narrow reasoning like this is distorting our thinking, not allowing us to see the bigger picture? So, let's look at the bigger picture. One obvious issue is that reducing class size requires more teachers. Can we make the assumption that the quality of these extra teachers will be as high? On further exploration this seems unlikely, given that these extra teachers might be the last ones into the profession, and might not otherwise have made the cut, or perhaps would have excluded themselves if class sizes were higher.

This single factor alone is a dynamic one, and a challenging subject. Look at it from another angle: if everything else is equal, schools advertising smaller classes might be paying their teachers less, thus demotivating teachers already working hard in the system. Or other trade-offs will be needed across the infrastructure or facilities, which is a double challenge given smaller class sizes means the need for more classrooms.

There are also benefits to bigger classes, which we could too easily disregard. For instance, a larger class will naturally have more energy and a livelier atmosphere, and there will be a greater chance of a student finding a peer whom they can learn from. Bigger classes also offer a better exposure to students from a range of backgrounds, which is relevant experience for our globally interconnected world. There is also the matter of stronger encouragement to learn self-direction skills.

Overall, the evidence does not show particularly large or clear effects until class size is reduced substantially, to fewer than 20 or 15 pupils.[64] It therefore appears difficult to achieve improvements in terms of progress of students from modest reductions in class size. The key issue is whether teachers are able to change their teaching approach, which is hard to do unless class sizes change by a lot. And even then there may well be much more effective ways of spending finite resources.

This is a broad finding, and there are other factors within it. For instance, some evidence suggests smaller classes have a slightly bigger impact for lower achievers and for very young children. But even then the impact falls short of what some of us would expect.

The point is not to send a message that class size doesn't matter, it is to try and explain that class size doesn't matter as much as we might think. The trap we can so easily fall into is paying too much attention to this single factor – frankly more than it deserves – because when we do that we are distracted from other important information.

Let's have a brief look at the other examples mentioned earlier, one of which was the presence of teaching assistants. The evidence is clear that teaching assistants can have a positive impact on academic achievement, but that the impact varies widely depending on whether they are providing general classroom support or whether they are supporting individual pupils or small groups.[65] Research looking at the impact of teaching assistants does not show a direct link between the amount of general classroom support and how well children do at school. Rather, it all depends on the deployment and how support is targeted. For instance, we know that when deployed well, teaching assistants can expand the variety of learning experiences provided. So again, this is an example of how narrowing down on a number can mask a wide range of other effects and perhaps mislead us.

Similarly, mentoring – pairing young people up with older peers or volunteers who can act as positive role models – appears on average to have little or no positive impact, on academic outcomes at least.[66] But again, the impact varies widely, and can look different for pupils from disadvantaged backgrounds or when the goal is to address attitudes, such as attendance and behaviour. In reality, it all comes down to how the mentoring relationships are structured, the expectations, the specific training of mentors, and the kind of support they get for what they do.

Finally, changes to the physical environment of schools or particular architecture is unlikely to dramatically affect the learning of children.[67] As part of a wider approach, such as connected to a whole-school change to establish new norms such as behaviour expectations, it can be effective as a catalyst for wider change, but alone makes little difference. The only substantial impact is seen at the extremes. For instance, if noise levels are very high, or the temperature is over 30 degrees, or humidity is excessive. As with the examples above, the results depend on a wide range of factors.

X AND Y

Education is inevitably complex, therefore we must be wary of any talk of silver bullets: to get a great education you need X or Y, for instance, as whatever you replace X or Y with will, at best, be only a small part of the answer.

Technology is another good example of why this particular X or Y shouldn't be a single deciding factor in education choices. Schools that advertise a distinct shift to online learning for certain tasks, or giving each child an iPad, could be considered as transformational; but in practice the evidence is mixed. As in so many other areas, there can be gains, but with considerable variation.[68] It is unlikely that any particular technology will bring about changes in learning directly, but it might if used to supplement teaching in the right way.

In reality, education is driven by many influences. Curriculum is important both in terms of the formal offer and enrichment opportunities; and academic performance is a key factor, including comparisons with other institutions in the area. Behaviour policy matters, not least because safety needs to be paramount. Other areas, such as facilities and services, might be important to you too; for instance, what happens at mealtimes or what out-of-hours programmes are available.

That is why Ofsted ratings[69] and performance table data[70] blend together a whole range of findings collected in a range of ways. There is no substitute for looking at information of that kind in the same way that there is no substitute for visits and seeking a range of views.

Decisions about education are all judgements to be made depending on the whole context rather than a single, narrow lens of focus, as a single factor will never provide the whole story of an education institution and its methods or approach. We must also consider that each child, young person or adult has their own needs, and tailoring education choices to those needs is important. The same applies once a child is in an education institution, and any talk of how X or Y are the standout answers to making progress should be considered with great caution.

In practice, education is based on complex human interactions. Similarly, there are no shortcuts. It shouldn't therefore come as a surprise that once a child or young person is at a school, involvement by parents at a relatively superficial level – such as attending events – is useful, but is not sufficient by itself to improve learning.[71]

Instead, in the early years and primary school, the kind of information needed by parents has more to do with the skills that are being worked on, tips for short and simple activities that can be done at home to back up what is being done at school, and support texts to provide encouragement and reinforcement.

At secondary school, more factual information specifically related to a child's progress, such as homework completion or updates about upcoming tasks, is required. For instance, a trial in secondary schools whereby parents received weekly messages over a year led to a month of additional progress for the young people involved. The texts informed about dates of upcoming tests, whether homework was submitted, and what young people were learning at school.

Ultimately, there is no substitute for one-to-one information with respect to the learning currently taking place. Any suggestion we can bypass that through a quick solution is probably too good to be true.

LOOKING AHEAD

With the overwhelming amount of information and data presented to us, the viewpoints of others around us, and our own thoughts, we can perhaps fall into the trap of rushing to come to a decision because of information overload.

The best course of action here is to slow down the decision-making process. Take time to look at a number of sources about an education institution, arrange to visit, talk to parents and students, meet the staff, read Ofsted reports, and look at websites or research reports.

And in the case of supporting progress and achievement, we are better off trying to continually understand how well a child or young person is doing at an individual level, connected directly to the learning that is happening, rather than relying on an isolated snapshot.

We are drawn to shortcuts, but should be wary of anything presented as "game-changing" as it might well end up falling short. Therefore, we need to take time to look at the many factors involved in education choices. By all means, zoom in to view details through a narrow lens, but zoom out too and look at the bigger picture.

Chapter Three

A QUESTION OF CHARACTER

More than any point in history it seems we are in need of people of great character; people who are resilient, committed, able to look beyond short-term pleasures; people who are honest, self-confident and with moral virtues.

We are living in a time of substantial global challenges. We need a collective response to climate change; conflicts still rage across the globe; billions worry about whether they will have enough food and water – and those are just some of the most pressing concerns today.[72] Tackling these problems requires specific expertise, and an understanding of how the world is changing, as well as all of the traits above.

We admire character when we see it: Nelson Mandela for his humility and ability to forgive; Winston Churchill for his dogged determination. But we don't admire those great leaders because of technical knowledge, or precise expertise, we admire them for their qualities.

We also look up to heroes around us who have shown tremendous character. Louis Rudd crossed 1,000 miles of Antarctica – the driest, coldest and most inhospitable place on the planet. Imagine how much determination and resilience that took, not to mention amazing courage after he lost a friend who died attempting the same challenge not long before.[73]

We also love hearing comeback stories of people who have survived the odds, because they inspire us and give us hope for our own lives. Abraham Lincoln was arguably one of the greatest American presidents, but he failed at business twice, had what would now be described as a nervous breakdown, and lost when running for the Congress and the Senate, and as a vice presidential candidate. Yet he went on to lead the country through the Civil War and abolished slavery.[74] Yes, we admire people when they just keep going, perhaps even more than we would have done had they achieved the same things the first time around.

When we think of our own friends and families and why we choose to spend time with them, it is often because of their character: their generosity, their openness, their kindness and their loyalty. We prize character highly, and what better opportunity to champion good character than within education? However, do we appreciate its value enough when it comes to education?

OUR DISLIKE OF AMBIGUITY

We are drawn to certainty and away from the unknown or things that feel vague or distant. This makes sense in many ways, particularly in a constantly changing world. A simple example is this: if offered a regular income each month versus an unknown payoff, then most people would go for the regular income.

An original example of preferring less ambiguous odds is the experiment where blindfolded people were asked to pick a ball from a container of red or green balls and then guess its colour. If they guessed correctly, they won money. One container had 50 red balls and 50 green balls, while another had a random proportion of both balls. Given the choice, most people chose the one with 50 balls of each colour, i.e. the option with the known probability (even though it offered no advantage at all.)[75]

Moving on to education, this could translate as being drawn to areas which are easy to understand, describe and measure because they feel like more probable bets. In academic terms, it is easy to picture what a maths or English lesson looks like, for instance, and how working hard to understand maths and achieve a good grasp of language can lead to better results and future success – and there is plenty of data available about maths and English stats. But when it comes to character education, how do we compare this with maths, English or science, for example, in terms of results and success?

We can too easily dismiss character education because our minds struggle to come up with examples of what such education might look like, or how it connects with the wider education system, especially when statements such as "flourishing lives" and "fulfilling potential" are relatively difficult to define.[76] There are many well-known measurements when it comes to academia; yet it seems we don't yet have such clear language to describe character.[77] Indeed, the debate is controversial and hotly contested,[78] as becoming a good person and a good citizen means different things to different people.

And there is an automatic part of our brains which concludes that a lack of "evidence" makes a choice feel risky in a "what works" culture.[79] Moreover, any benefits of character development can seem distant; for instance, the benefits of living a well-rounded life can sometimes seem a long way off.

Another issue is whilst there can be a lot of appreciation for various character-building school activities, from sport to musical performance to volunteering, there can be a lack of engagement from both parents and pupils.[80] There is also the question of prioritisation to consider. For instance, a survey of parents showed that a good knowledge of key subjects was seen as much more important than developing attributes like relating to others or empathy.[81] It seems that academic subjects still receive a much greater focus.[82]

Next time you visit a friend or relative with a new-born baby, ask them what they want for their child. More often than not you will get the same answer: "To be happy." But ask the parents 16 years later what they want for him or her, and the answer is often different. Hopes and aspirations change and become more complex over time; and things which didn't seem to matter so much before suddenly matter a lot later on, especially when it comes to academic achievement. In fact, at least one survey suggests getting good results overtakes happiness as the top parental concern.[83] There's no one reason for that. It is the culmination of mindsets and attitudes.

EMERGING EVIDENCE

Of course, the focus on getting good academic results is entirely sensible. The modern workplace is highly competitive, and good results can be a gateway to options and experiences that might otherwise be closed off. These, in turn, often lead to greater security and prosperity.

But there are obvious benefits too to character development, given that young people will grow up and will need to be able to choose the right course of action in difficult situations, and make wise choices about how they live, cooperate and work with others.

Crucially, this need not actually be an either/or.

In fact, evidence suggests that character education can contribute to how well children do academically,[84] not least because children with better wellbeing so often do better anyway.[85] Indeed, character education is associated with a range of positive outcomes in school – including impact on tangible results such as reading and maths scores.[86] This is especially true for those from a more disadvantaged background for whom "resilience factors", such as confidence and self-esteem, are associated with achieving more academically.[87]

There are few better examples than Albert Einstein. "You're no Einstein," has become a common remark about intelligence. Indeed, the man has become a benchmark of intelligence and academic ability. But his path to success was based on much more than intelligence. Einstein was named *Time* magazine's Person of the Century for traits of character.[88] In his own words: "*Most people say that it is the intellect which makes a great scientist. They are wrong: it is character.*"

In many ways Einstein was deeply flawed, so he is far from an example of perfect character, if such a thing exists. But he showed persistence after making mistakes, commitment to spending decades researching and defending his work, determination to take on more and more difficult challenges, and resilience in overcoming difficulties such as poor memory and struggling with some subjects at school.[89]

Building on this, surveys show that the majority of employers value these kinds of skills and traits as much as qualifications.[90] If you doubt any of that, think back to people you were at school with. I would be surprised if you can't think of those who didn't do that well academically, but have gone on to succeed anyway.

There is evidence that character attributes are associated with better life outcomes,[91] including things like financial stability in adulthood and reduced crime. To take a specific finding – one of many – higher levels of conscientiousness in children is strongly linked with outcomes in adulthood around employment and wage returns.[92]

Similarly, self-control is a skill which has been shown to be important in various studies, including some of the most thorough; for example, one by researchers which has been tracking a cohort of children for many years.[93] We can measure self-control by asking about and testing impulse and self-regulation. It is possible to then explore association with outcomes later in life. The findings are striking across both social and financial outcomes.

Other character traits have been proven to be even more valuable. A ground-breaking study concerning the need for children to develop "grit" – in other words, passion and perseverance for long-term goals – suggests success and fulfilment depends on it, and it can be more important than great talent which, by itself, is wasted if people don't have enough stamina.[94] And these are just some findings.

One of the reasons this area is so important is that different things will work for different young people. Some might need to develop compassion for others, or learn how to become more confident, or how to be responsible citizens. Varying backgrounds, cohorts and cultures will mean tailored strategies and interventions can have substantial impact if deployed in the right way.[95]

GROWING UP TODAY

The evidence that character education done well has enormous potential, especially given the challenges of modern-day life, is powerful. We want young people to grow up to be active and responsible citizens who try things out, meet people, see and do, contribute to society and respect differences; and everyone should be able to enjoy and appreciate the wonders of the world around them and lead a fulfilling life.

Say that to a teenager growing up in Britain today and it might sound like a tall order, however. Everyone has a tendency to think life was better in their day. But whether this is true or not, many of us would agree that life isn't as easy as it could be for young people today.

You only need to open a newspaper to get a sense of some of the possible challenges. Around one in 10 young people in the UK often feel lonely, especially around times of transition such as moving from primary to secondary school.[96] Around 75% of adult mental health problems begin before the age of 18, and the children's commissioner has warned about mental health needs, and how providing help when problems emerge in childhood would reap benefits when youngsters enter adulthood.[97]

The trend that saddens me the most is the proportion of young people who said they had someone to rely on has decreased.[98] Anxiety and depression are up. Stress has got to the point where some universities are offering dog walking and colouring books to relieve it.[99]

The good news is that there are already organisations across the country, such as Guides and Scouts and the Duke of Edinburgh Award, which recognise that the route to success today is as much about what is inside as it is about any qualifications we hold or academic knowledge we have attained. Of course, qualifications and an academic education matter a lot, but time and energy spent developing character doesn't take away from those things, it adds to them, and helps equip young people to flourish in modern Britain and face down the challenges that will inevitably come their way.

To take one example, the National Citizen Service brings young people together to undertake personal and social development, and community action. Nearly half a million have taken part, and the clear majority left more confident about getting a job, more positive about people from different backgrounds, and with better satisfaction and lower anxiety.[100]

Similarly, taking part in the cadets has a positive correlation with personal and social development, key skills and employability.[101] Evidence shows extra-curricular activity leads to increases in young people's views of their own social and emotional skills.[102] School leaders report that sport instils qualities such as determination, self-discipline and team spirit.[103]

And there are ambitious new initiatives, such as the School Games building on the 2012 Olympics, with a key focus on every child participating in meaningful competition. We have a new activity passport for children in primary schools in England, which includes getting soaking wet by year two, making a sculpture by year four, and seeing the sun rise by year six.[104]

But whilst trials and programmes provide encouraging evidence, this is a complex agenda. We need to know more about how character is developed through education, and even then no two people will develop in the same way, so we must learn how best to take into account individual and contextual differences.

This is an area we need to dig into much more to find the best interventions, and there are a lot of promising areas to explore further. For instance, sharing examples of lives lived well could inspire others; training people to perform following hours of rehearsal could show that there are no shortcuts; teaching how to master a skill could help people build commitment and dedication. There are other factors too: developing deep knowledge and understanding builds self-confidence; when you are part of a group you learn how to take pride in achievements and abide by the rules; work in the community builds generosity; and dealing with wins and losses helps us be "gracious in victory and humble in defeat".

There are exciting new studies taking place. One new area is mindfulness, which helps people focus on the present moment while acknowledging and accepting thoughts, feelings and bodily sensations. A trial is happening at the moment to see if mindfulness improves self-control.

Work is also underway to explore the virtues which underpin good character education, including honesty, self-control, fairness, resilience and respect. The idea is to develop a stronger shared understanding of the role these virtues play in helping both individuals and society to flourish, so that we then stand a better chance of implementing character education in a meaningful and impactful way.[105]

LOOKING AHEAD

One powerful thing we can each do is remember that we are naturally drawn towards certainty and therefore results, data and measurement. Academic education aligns well with that tendency. But character programmes and interventions can be just as valuable, even if they are inevitably harder to pin down. We can seek clarity in other ways; for example, focusing on the end goals, such as wanting to prepare young people for life's inevitable knocks, because we know that developing self-belief drives us on, and improving tenacity helps us stick with the tasks at hand.

Collectively, we can work at breaking through the ambiguity around character education so that we are better able to make informed choices. For instance, the Jubilee Centre for Character and Virtues is taking forward work to set up a framework and benchmarks to illustrate what good character education looks like.

But an environment for children and young people focused on making them well-rounded individuals ready for the modern world and all its challenges will inevitably look different for different people and in different places. In this area, research and evidence will only take us so far, and much of it is about our own prioritisation. The bottom line is that when it comes to fulfilling potential and living flourishing lives, character matters as much as anything else.

Part Two

OUR OWN PATH

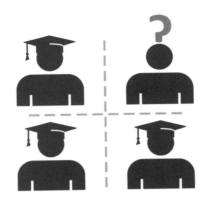

Chapter Four

VOCATIONAL SNOBBERY

Many aspects of modern life can be traced back to one of the most defining periods of western history: the Industrial Revolution.[106] How we travel, communicate, bank and trade were all transformed during this period. Britain's role was pivotal, and there are various reasons for that. One of them was that we had a lot of coal; but a more interesting development was that much of the inspirational thinking and invention stemmed from Britain. For that to happen, we needed the right climate for those ideas to then take off, which they did.[107] But climate alone was not enough: we needed the people to come up with the ideas in the first place.

One of the striking things about many of the people who came up with these remarkable inventions is that they didn't have the kind of education that you might guess. James Watt built the steam engine, but he didn't attend school regularly. What he excelled at was manual dexterity rather than Greek or Latin, and he learnt by making and repairing telescopes and barometers, amongst other things.[108] Isambard Kingdom Brunel built the Great Western railway, steamships, bridges and tunnels; but having been rejected from a renowned engineering school, he honed his skills during an apprenticeship.[109] Richard Arkwright created the modern factory system; but his parents couldn't afford to send him to school, so he was apprenticed, and began working life as a barber and a wig-maker.[110]

That people learn by actually doing things has always been true. The system of apprenticeships has existed in the UK since the Middle Ages, when parents sent their children to live with host families and learn craft guilds.[111] The first national apprenticeship scheme began in 1563 by the Elizabethan Statute of Artificers (skilled craftsman), when masters had no more than three apprentices and apprenticeships lasted seven years. But views have changed.

THE BANDWAGON

We pay a lot of attention to what other people think, and if others are doing something we are often inclined to do it too; and the more people who adopt a particular trend, the more likely it becomes that other people will also hop on the bandwagon.[112] There are a variety of drivers, which can involve pressure to conform with what others around us are doing, a desire to be part of the winning side, and a need to feel included rather than be the odd one out.

When we reflect on our own choices, we can usually recognise this thinking bias. We might begin wearing a style of clothes because we have seen others adopt the same fashion. Music increases in popularity when more and more people start listening to it. And when increasing numbers of people start using social media sites, others are more likely to start using them as well – and when it comes to social media, "influencers" increasingly drive consumption trends.

There are benefits to this approach. For instance, we are more likely to embrace healthy choices if others do, or reject smoking if only a small minority of people around us smoke. But we also need to be wary of this form of thinking bias. For instance, people are more likely to vote for the candidate in an election they think is winning.[113]

Moving on to education, the ingredients for the bandwagon effect can be present. Higher education is an example. There is a strong sense that university is the obvious next step for those with the right grades; and for young people themselves, if many of their friends and peers are going to university, then it's so often easier to go with the norms and attitudes of the majority.

There are advantages to this approach and, for many, higher education is a brilliant option, and the widening participation agenda across higher education has done tremendous amounts to spread opportunity. There has certainly been huge expansion: student numbers have almost doubled since 1992,[114] and university applications have again hit record numbers.[115] But what about the alternatives?

"VOCATIONAL" – A DIRTY WORD?

The honest truth is that we do have a social

narrative in our country that says educational success at university leads to a high economic status career, and is a main marker of self-esteem. The big problem is that this can make us snobs about vocational education. Evidence shows that 65% of teachers would rarely or never recommend an apprenticeship to students if they could go to university, and only one quarter of parents judge vocational education to be worthwhile.[116] Students themselves have the greatest knowledge and awareness of university, and many university students, when asked about their decisions, explained that their schools had seen university as the default option.[117] Indeed, over 36% of parents do not even know what an apprenticeship is, and we know that parents and family members have the biggest influence on study aspirations.[118]

Sadly, we do not seem to have an image in our minds of teenagers running down the stairs telling us they just got into college to study a vocational course like we do for those getting into a university; and not everyone pictures celebrating the completion of an apprenticeship in the same way as we might celebrate someone getting onto a competitive graduate programme. In this respect, the word "vocational" has almost become a dirty word: we don't use it for anything we hold in high regard, such as medicine, even if it is vocational in nature.

We didn't always think like this. Each human life has unique value, and each person makes a valuable contribution. While intelligence and academic achievement are to be admired, we used to make it easier for people to take pride in training in other ways – including mastering a craft skill, building up physical strength and endurance for tough jobs, or developing the dedication to serving others around them.

In a country of such rich intellectual heritage – the country of Shakespeare, David Hume, and Adam Smith, with the oldest university in the English-speaking world, and some of the most famous public schools in the world – it was always a risk that we might lean too much in that direction. It was only in the 1950s that Oxford and Cambridge Universities stopped requiring students to have qualifications in Latin.[119]

In this context, our bias runs wider and deeper than we might have expected, given we are also the country of Watt, Brunel and Arkwright. Many of us are guilty of this bias, and we are often well-meaning. When Michelle Obama spoke at a London school, she didn't consciously do down technical education, but she spoke most passionately about her Ivy League education and how others here could overcome their own doubters and naysayers to achieve similar aspirations.[120]

THE NUANCED REALITY

To be clear, for many a traditional university degree will be a great choice and going down that path could well be the best thing to do. On average, graduate earnings are higher,[121] and a degree opens up a range of post-graduate qualifications which are otherwise inaccessible.[122] Besides, education at this level can be a wonderful experience.

More broadly, our universities can lead to wider society benefits, too. They attract global talent,[123] and build international connections; indeed, a substantial proportion of countries have a leader who studied in the UK.[124] As significant investors, universities can help regenerate an area.[125] And, more widely, they can enhance self-knowledge, employment opportunities and civil participation.[126]

The picture, though, is rather more nuanced than we may initially think, so let's look at this from an individual perspective, because what others

do is useful for us to consider, but not necessarily the best determinant of what we should
do ourselves. The latest data from the Office of
National Statistics shows that almost a third of
graduates are overqualified for the job they are
doing, especially students of the arts, biology
and humanities.[127] And looking through the latest
data about happiness and wellbeing, the key
drivers tend to be in areas such as health, social
connection and relationships.[128] There is considerable evidence that work as opposed to unemployment is important, and our financial position
matters if we are otherwise on the margins of
poverty; but there isn't a compelling case that
particular qualifications or a particular level of
education stands out as a driver for happiness.

Crucially, there are alternative routes available,
particularly vocational education. Many young
people will have a sense of the occupations they
are interested in pursuing, and often the best route
will be to train directly for them, using valuable
time to develop the technical knowledge, skills
and behaviours to become qualified professionals. This can include occupations ranging
from programmers to police officers to sports
therapists.

Some people are better suited to contextual
learning and the kind of course where they

can see a direct line between their efforts and a specific occupation or career. For some, it is more motivating if the learning is "authentic" and focused on the real world.[129] Research shows that a particularly important aspect of vocational education is the meaningful contextualisation in a variety of different ways, including in the workplace, so that it is clear how what is being learnt is relevant to future jobs.[130] And one of the unique features of high quality vocational education, which is not prevalent elsewhere, is exposure to up-to-date industry experiences, facilities and expertise.[131]

Critically, the returns to the best technical education courses are very healthy. Evidence shows that there is a significant wage return for most vocational qualifications, with proof of a positive return at all levels. There is a strong association, too, with likelihood of employment for all types and levels of vocational qualifications.[132] And technical courses and apprenticeships go up to the higher levels – some all the way up to the equivalent level of full academic degrees.

What is more, there is a growing consensus that we need a level playing field, and for all young people to have a genuine choice about their education. Therefore, more needs to be done to ensure that all vocational options are every bit as attractive as any academic alternative.

THE VALUE OF VOCATIONAL EDUCATION

We can all play a role by having real appreciation for vocational education. We need to reset what we think of it, how we intuitively respond to it, and therefore the choices we make. To do that, we can start by getting to the bottom of what it really is rather than the skewed impression we can so easily have of it.

You could live your whole life taking an interest in the lives of others, and being curious about everything around us, without ever hearing a fair explanation of what vocational education actually is. Instead, we can too easily absorb a definition of what it isn't: an academic education achieved by going to university.

But we don't describe the west of England by saying it is not the east. We don't describe elderly people by saying they are the opposite of young. We don't describe classical music by starting with a description of pop music and then setting out the things that are different about it. We owe to all of those things – and the people whose identities are linked to them – a fair description of what they are *in their own right*, so why not show the same respect to vocational education?

Learning from international evidence, vocational education is for those who wish to gain the technical knowledge and skills needed for specific types of skilled employment. The first thought might be to do that job by job, but that wouldn't get us very far. "Jobs" in fact have quite limited meanings, because they are focused on specific employment contracts in specific workplaces, so a "job description" can be just a list of tasks that an individual might perform. An "occupation" is something different, however, in that it is broader and more substantial; it allows us to look at someone's profession, consider the skills requirements, and map how progression and promotion works.

We could look at all the occupations in the economy, based on the current labour market and predictions about future skills needs, and group them together based on similarities.[133] For instance, conservationists have overlapping skills with horticulturalists and agricultural managers, but much less overlap with graphic designers; graphic designers have much in common with clothing designers, tailors and furniture makers, but are completely different to paralegals. And so on.

Having the groupings allows us to design training which is valued by industry, in a way which gives people transferable skills, but avoids the risk of trying to cover off such a wide area that training is too general to be useful. We can look at the technical knowledge, practical skills and behaviours which suit each group of occupations. For instance, in construction you would need to know construction standards, engineering principles, how to comply with health and safety guidance, etc. First training could therefore cover core content, and then specialise towards specific occupations.

It is only worth taking that approach where there is a large enough body of content, however. Some occupations can be learnt in a few weeks, once in the job, and anything more is overkill. Some occupations are at the other end of the spectrum and require (at least) an undergraduate degree to cover the full volume of knowledge. What is left represents millions and millions of roles in our economy,[134] so we really must get our thinking right on this.

The absolutely critical principle is that training needs to be guided by employers; but employers continue to say that many people who have successfully completed qualifications are poorly equipped to start skilled work with them. So, they need to set the standards. That can happen either in an employment-based way – most commonly apprenticeships – or on college-based courses, which are typically full-time courses with work placements. Both are equally valid as long as they work backwards from what employers want.

Leading international countries have put employers in the driving seat for years. Denmark, for example, has trade committees which define and develop vocational qualifications, and they are then backed by the state, which upholds overall standards and makes sure that qualifications are reliable and robust.[135]

Another thing which sets excellent vocational education apart in the best international examples is the opportunity to develop skills in real-life environments. So, an aspiring engineer could see what project sites are really like, see for themselves the kinds of day-to-day behaviours that would be expected from them, and put into practice some of the technical knowledge they have built up. For apprentices, there is plenty of chance to do that, and for college-based courses, work placements are vital.

Finally, the best vocational education is a lifelong thing, with pathways available at all ages and points. Adults have the same choices as young people, either moving on to them directly if they have the prerequisite knowledge and skills, or doing so via appropriate access, support or bridging arrangements.[136]

That summary describes what the best vocational training looks like. If we get it right, millions of people will be better placed to choose the right path for themselves and thrive. Care workers will give the best support possible to those in society most in need. Coastguards will rescue as many people as they possibly can. Probation officers will rehabilitate countless lives. When they thrive, we all thrive.

In countries where vocational education is prioritised, everyone benefits, and the whole country is better off. We can learn from them. Germany, one of our main international competitors, is a good example. Rivalry is a funny thing. When it comes to football, in the run up to a big match the English press will print articles running through previous encounters, and often remind us of our 1966 glory at the World Cup, even though the Germans have won four World Cups to our one. Millions across the country are horrified if we lose a football match to Germany, but in the words of Gary Lineker: "*Football is a simple game; 22 men chase a ball for 90 minutes and, at the end, the Germans win.*"

Sadly, that outcome applies to another part of national life: every day Germany outdoes us when it comes to productivity and how they train their young people for the future. A revealing feature is how much of a shared responsibility vocational education is – across federal government, regions, employers, unions and sector bodies ("chambers") – and those chambers then draw on a range of expertise, including teachers, and are tasked with continuous development of quality.[137] We could learn a lot from that.

This is far from the first time that a collective need to focus more on vocational education has been raised. Sir Bernhard Samuelson – an ironmaster by trade – gave expert advice to Parliament about the importance of technical instruction. In 1881, he was appointed chairman of a royal commission on technical instruction. As a result, the government went as far as raising duty on beer and spirits for the assistance of technical education.[138] That probably isn't the answer this time, but what hasn't changed is the sense of shared endeavour and responsibility that is needed.

LOOKING AHEAD

Let's remind ourselves that we have a tendency

to follow others, and that this isn't necessarily related to the quality of the option they have chosen, or what may be right for us, but instead our human nature; and jumping on the bandwagon may seem like the obvious approach, but that doesn't take into account that we are individuals, with our own needs and preferences, and a different path may be better.

In the case of higher education and vocational education, it is helpful to seek a number of different views and look at the objective evidence. University can be a brilliant path, but more and more the high quality apprenticeships and technical courses are worth a look as well, especially if you want line of sight to a particular profession, advanced training on the job, and strong employer and business support.

Finally, we must all champion the skills of millions of people employed in the occupations which keep our country moving forwards, including occupations which require substantial training but are not suited to degrees at university, such as farmers, chefs, IT technicians and nursing assistants. Only then will training for those roles be seen as equally important; and only then will we match the best in the world.

Chapter Five

SKEWED SUCCESS STORIES

When people make the most of their potential, amazing things can happen. It took those at the edge of their abilities to make some of the most important advances in modern medicine, bring the Internet to life, and land a spacecraft on Mars. But, for much of Britain's history, most people would have been shut out from getting anywhere near those kinds of achievements as, traditionally, so many people grew up thinking they had a station in life based on their background.

We can therefore celebrate that we have, at least by historic standards, broken free – and that isn't just good for the individuals involved, we all benefit. Scientific and technological advances help us all, and so does the more equal society that is created when people are not constrained by their circumstances. For each of 11 different health and social problems, including physical health, drug abuse, imprisonment, obesity, trust and community life, to name a few, outcomes are significantly worse in more unequal countries.[139]

But when we think about prospects, and the likelihood of success, our minds couldn't possibly analyse all the information and evidence, so we tend to reach for a limited pool of examples which come to mind, without realising we often attach undue weight to those examples. For instance, for people who only know those who've had negative experiences, that can be dangerous, because it can lead to the belief that success is pre-determined. They can also give far too much weight to assumed results. Therefore, it is common to hear things like: "Well, I was never good at maths, so it's no surprise that my daughter isn't either," at parents' evenings.

Much energy over recent decades has been spent challenging that kind of assumption, and we need to continue to do so. And we know that while results vary, many studies have struggled to demonstrate that more than a small per cent of differences in education results can be predicted based on genetics.[140] Genetics or circumstance, therefore, are not automatic predictors of an individual's ability.

But even for those of us who can draw on a range of influences which are not skewed in this way, is there another issue at play? We don't just recall the examples of friends and family who we have relationships with, we also bring to mind examples of people who we don't know, and that can lead to a different kind of problem.

SURVIVORSHIP BIAS

We have a bias in our thinking towards survivors – and by that we mean we pay most attention to the people or things that made it past a certain barrier rather than those that failed to do so. Famously, this thinking bias has been illustrated through the example of fighter planes in the Second World War.

Unsurprisingly, many planes were lost in combat and, for the planes which came back, the intuitive response was to keep track of any that got hit and made it back to see where the bullet holes were, so that they could then reinforce the planes in the vulnerable positions. Later on, though, the survivorship bias was pointed out: if a plane could get hit in those positions and make it back, they weren't the vulnerable points, after all – it was the rest of the plane that needed reinforcement.[141]

To use another example, it is often said that music was better in the 1960s, or that cars aren't made the way they used to be. Again, this is survivorship bias at play. Yes, the Beatles and the Rolling Stones were pretty special, but they were not representative of all music from that decade, because we've simply forgotten about most of it. Similarly with cars, the Ford Thunderbird, Austin Mini and Chevrolet Corvette are impressive pieces of engineering from the 1950s, but they stand out because the less remarkable cars from that time have faded from view.

We think the same way when it comes to our own lives. Stories about the world's oldest people tend to come with advice about how they reached such an impressive age, and naturally we listen to it in the hope of learning something. But are the following really the answers: playing cards, drinking a glass of dry white wine before meals, two raw eggs a day, eating bacon every morning, or never getting into a relationship?[142]

We might be better off learning what not to do!

Moving on to education, when we think about a particular path or career or profession, we are biased towards thinking about the people who have been most successful, and those who failed to make it big tend to either get less attention, or are completely ignored. The temptation is then to try and follow the survivors – the big success stories – deconstructing their success and looking for clues in what they did which we can copy ourselves.

SUCCESS STORIES

When we look at the availability and visibility of advice, the winners do seem to have the monopoly. Any bookshop is full of self-help books on subjects such as "thinking big", "positive mental attitude", and "how to have the best year of your life", generally written by people who have reached a particular status and can reflect back.

Celebrities, when asked about their success, happily advise others, and often focus on messages such as "believe in yourself", and that "if you can dream it you can do it". For instance, Lionel Messi, arguably one of the greatest footballers ever, talks about the sacrifices he made to achieve his dreams as if his journey can apply to us all.[143] But we can never know if doing exactly what these super-successful people did would work again, or indeed what role luck or circumstance played in their lives. There will be numerous others who tackled the journey in the same way but who disappeared from view, or simply aren't visible to us because they're not as big as "the greats".

The inspirational examples often told to young people are about role models who put in the sweat and sacrifice to eventually make it. We think there's a risk young people don't understand the importance of maximizing their potential and working hard, that they think things come easy in life, and don't need to put the effort in.

It is often the most successful people who are asked to go back into schools to give inspiring talks, who are interviewed in the media for advice to others, and who are paid to write books and go on lecture circuits. In fact, it's very hard to get accounts from the people who tried and failed, and when you search online you tend to hear from the people who stumbled first and then made it big, which is not the same as never making it at all.

It's not that we want to keep talking about failure, it's just that only looking at the "big" stories can mean young people are disproportionately exposed to the experiences and journeys of a small number of highly successful people only. We are all drawn to those big cases for a reason, because they prove "big" can still be done; but this means that a limited range of examples make a big impression, and can be given a lot of attention and emphasis, whilst ignoring everyone else.

We see this playing out a lot. Moving beyond the individual view and looking at the aggregate impact, a survey of the career aspirations of thousands of English teenagers showed they selected their preferred future jobs from a narrow pool of jobs that represented only 34% of the roles that will be available in the future.[144] Some findings were striking. For instance, for teenagers age 15-16, 21% have ambitions to secure the 2.4% of the jobs in culture, media and sport.[145]

REALISTIC PATHS

We can learn a lot from the success stories, especially the underlying messages about hard work and commitment, which are essential. But *each* specific story or group of stories only helps to a certain extent, and often need caution and caveats if young people are going to then try and learn directly from them when determining their own paths.

Take Michael Phelps – arguably one of the greatest swimmers – as another example. He encourages us all to dream more to achieve more: *"There will be obstacles. There will be doubters. There will be mistakes. But with hard work, there are no limits."*[146] But is "there are no limits" really good advice?

No one can deny how hard he works, but he is called the "Flying Fish" for a reason: he is six feet four inches tall – apparently the ideal height for swimming! – with size 14 feet! And most strikingly of all, his wingspan is three inches more than his height, which is very unusual (in fact, his torso matches that of someone who is six feet eight inches tall). Simply put, he is not an ordinary person. He has an unusual body shape, which gives him tremendous advantage when it comes to pulling himself through the water.[147] Therefore, the advice he gives may not apply well to others who don't share the same physical attributes.

Moving on to a different case, when The Sunday Times Rich List comes out each year, one of the first ways it is cut is to explore the number of people who left education with no qualifications but then became a billionaire. Each time there are examples of entrepreneurial business people: Simon Dolan, Lee Biggins and Oliver Cookson, for instance.[148] When interviewed, they naturally talk about their own journeys and how, for them, not pursuing further qualifications was the right option.

But while those stories might seem to offer lessons that many others could follow, they are really the exceptions rather than the rule. Moving beyond a sample of only three people (in a country of over 65 million), the overwhelming evidence says that education is a key predictor of success, including for entrepreneurs,[149] and so you are most likely to be better off if you *don't* follow their example.

As another illustration, we are particularly fond of hearing about people who we consider self-made successes, and have overcome tough circumstances to do well against the odds; or, to use the common phrase: "People who pulled themselves up by their bootstraps." Arnold Schwarzenegger, for example, scraped money together bricklaying before becoming a businessman and then movie star. But, in practice, the idea of being able to pull yourself up by your bootstraps tends to only extend so far; and as well as only being a small subset of the relevant examples out there, "rags to riches" stories are often crunched down so much that by the time they reach us they are distorted at best, or inaccurate at worst.

People who have gone from "rags to riches" usually had help along the way, but accounts of their success often neglect to give that help enough credit. Arnold Schwarzenegger was encouraged to play several sports at school, which he attributes to his early success at weight training; whilst support to train at the local gym and to study psychology (to learn more about the power of mind over body) set him on a path to bodybuilding success.[150]

These are rare cases, and the bigger picture does look different. Social mobility has, at best, stayed constant since the 1980s, and the UK is one of the lowest performing developed countries for income mobility.[151] For many – although there are exceptions – an ongoing issue is access to education and job opportunities, and, in practice, there are asymmetries both in terms of information and networks.

Finally, institutions are naturally drawn to high-lighting their "survivors". Schools, colleges and universities will often market themselves based on their most famous alumni (or at least the alumni they are most proud to be associated with), and providers of qualifications and courses will do the same. To use one example, there are many creative arts courses available, and many examples of hugely talented people who have attended these courses; but it will be the stunning successes of recent graduates that are used for advertising purposes. It is also relevant that average earnings for creative arts graduates is right at the lower end of the spectrum compared with other subjects; in fact, typically a quarter less than average graduates, and significant differences remain once student characteristics are taken into account. Marketing isn't always representative.[152]

In truth, the reality can look rather different to the success stories. For instance, the top five jobs that 16- to 21-year-olds aspired to all showed a decline when compared with actual numbers of 22- to 29-year-olds in those occupations.[153] As well as unrealistic prospects, in focusing solely on the survivors and their stories we are missing a huge source of information: advice on what not to do, or what we should avoid because it didn't work out. Information like that is lost, which is a great shame, because learning about how to avoid obvious mistakes, or realising that sometimes a path might not be the thing we're looking for – for instance, not to choose one course if we have skills more suited to another – could be very useful, and save us a lot of time and energy.

There is a human cost to this mismatch. We know that when young people have a misalignment between ambitions and the realistic paths available to them they are much less likely to make a smooth transition to work. The risk is also high that young people will find they have developed skills profiles which lead to them "churning" in the labour market as they then try to get additional training and experience.[154]

At an aggregate level, this matters greatly, because a mismatch of information to skills is a real problem in a global competitive world, where we need to invest in our people, who will then drive innovation and harness technology and continue to create and advance companies in the 21st century.

THINKING BIG

This is not to say that we don't want young people to dream big, or that success stories are not inspirational. Aspiration is hugely powerful, and belief in our ability to succeed can impact on whether we actually do go on to succeed. Indeed, our most basic beliefs matter a lot, and our mindset propels us forward and helps determine whether or not we will fulfil our potential. We want people to have growth mindsets.[155] The hand we were dealt at first is just the starting point for future development, and with the right attitudes we can go on and thrive. But it doesn't do anyone any favours to set out on unrealistic paths, or follow advice based on just one or two journeys out of the many thousands of journeys we can learn from.

Some people will make it as they intended, and others will be happy in a different occupation within a field they are passionate about, but may not have initially seen themselves pursuing. What is true is that the great majority of people will benefit from the right kind of advice to make informed decisions about the future.

In practice, we know that means being able to access information about careers and the labour market, understanding how curriculum and study links to careers and the world of work, having encounters with employers, experiencing the workplace directly, and getting some tailored advice. New Gatsby benchmarks for good careers advice are now available,[156] and there are various organisations such as the Careers and Enterprise Company which can provide further guidance.[157]

There is compelling evidence to suggest that learning about careers needs to start at primary school and continue through into adulthood. The way teenagers think about their futures determines what happens in later life, and young people who underestimate the education required for desired professions are sadly more likely to end up unemployed.[158]

There is actually some brilliant advice across the country now: local businesses going into schools and colleges to do assemblies and to provide work placements; education institutions making careers advice not just a tick-box exercise but rather part of the whole culture; and talented advisers meeting students directly to share expertise, improve employer engagement, and ensure young people hear about new skills and opportunities which could otherwise be completely invisible.

Critically, we each need a well-rounded view, and a handful of experiences may be a useful contribution but are far from the whole guide. We need to understand enough about the world of work to know what skills are needed to succeed, and we need to be able to witness careers for real to know they exist and learn how to get there.

LOOKING AHEAD

It helps us all to remember that we have a thinking bias towards the survivors and believing that what they say is representative advice. It simply is not, and every spectacular success story needs to be taken with a pinch of salt and balanced with a more realistic example of what success looks like. In short, if anyone is basing their career paths and goals only on the big success stories, big warning bells should sound.

That doesn't mean that we can't encourage big aspirations and a belief in maximising potential. We all, young people included, get one chance at life, and we want them to aim high and find areas they are passionate about. High expectations have driven so many successes around the world, both individually and collectively, and will carry on being one of the most influential drivers.

We need to combine that with practical support. It will look different at different stages, but there is no substitute for multiple opportunities to hear about the world of work, spending time in it, hearing about the full range of options available, and receiving some personalised support tailored towards individual aspirations and needs. Talking openly about a young person's future should be the baseline they deserve. Few things are as important as preparing and inspiring young people for the world of work.

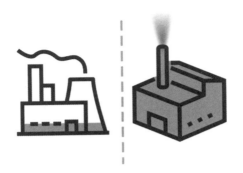

Chapter Six

THE SHIFTING STATUS QUO

The modern workplace is unrecognisable compared to only a few decades ago. One of the main drivers of change has been technology: you can now wear a device on your wrist that works out how many calories you have burnt and whether you've had enough sleep; you can connect with innumerable people via multiple platforms to work and socialise and communicate; you can leave a restaurant and instantly book a personalised journey home from your exact location. (And it is already outdated to talk about how the GPS systems once designed for fighter pilots now help us complete everyday journeys.)

Further change is coming. Soon there will be vehicles which can drive and navigate without humans. Systems are getting better and better at collecting and analysing data without needing human input. More and more software can perceive its environment, control actions and adapt accordingly.

We would expect this to improve our productivity, and some estimates put the impact on the labour market in line with the effect of the steam engine in Britain, but the changes will be far quicker.[159] Changes in technology can happen in ways we wouldn't quite expect. For example, when cash machines were introduced in the USA there was a parallel expansion in the employment of bank tellers. This was because more ATMs led to more bank branches, which then meant more tellers were needed to do the things that cash machines couldn't.[160] Similarly, the railways initially led to greater demand for horse-drawn carriages, because in some places the increase of people arriving by train meant a greater need for a carriage for the final part of their journey.[161]

The changes we are experiencing make the world of work a very exciting place. Many jobs available now didn't exist a few years ago; podcast producers, cloud architects, and automated driving engineers, to name a few. And technology helps create jobs in other ways by driving economic growth; for example, 3D printing increases manufacturing capacity, and access to the Internet means that when someone somewhere in the world creates a new business idea or product, we all have much quicker access to it. But if this is such an opportunity, why is it easy to also be anxious about it?

THE STATUS QUO

Our brains have a thinking bias towards maintaining the status quo, and we have an inbuilt preference for how things currently are. As a result, when change does happen we can intuitively view it through the prism of what we are losing, or the detriment it causes, rather than the gains and benefits.

Simply put, we like things to stay the same. We find change hard, and it can happen so fast. Just take the high street as an example. Most of us can remember going to Woolworths for pick 'n' mix sweets, Blockbuster to rent a video tape to watch on Saturday night, and to Dixons, which was once "the future" of electrical goods. Once proud retailers have been reduced to nothing. We tend to look back on them fondly, and miss their familiarity.

A number of experiments have proved this bias in our thinking.[162] Sticking with established brands is an example: in blind testing, the preference for strong brands like Coca Cola is much lower than when people are able to see the brands and choose the ones they recognise.[163] In Germany, a town had to be relocated, and residents chose to build it in a very similar way to before, despite its inefficient layout.[164]

We also recognise such behaviours in the way that we go about our lives. Every time we visit our favourite restaurant we often default towards the same choices on the menu, even though a new dish might be even better. Utility providers know that once we have signed up with a company we are more likely to stick with them, even if there are better and cheaper options available. Looking at our finances, we often keep money in relatively low interest earning accounts rather than move it to get better financial rewards.

Moving on to education, and by extension the workplace, the status quo bias can make us more attached to a particular career path we have set out on and less keen on a possible change of direction. Like the other thinking biases, there are benefits to this approach: we should be wary about taking unnecessary risks; there are big advantages to seeing something through; and sticking with what we know does offer some degree of protection and stabilisation. But not always.

When we think about changing our skillset and retraining, we can weigh quite heavily in our minds what we might lose, and we can easily build up "what-if" scenarios in our minds, wondering about all the things that could go wrong if we step out into other fields. Our brains can focus disproportionately on the sunk cost – the time and effort we have put in to get to where we are today – and less on the potential rewards of retraining. And we can give the short-term costs great weight compared with the long-term gains.

We are also creatures of habit. We like to have a script which we replay again and again, and our jobs, as they stand today, can help us do that. And we can naturally look more towards what is happening inside our own lives rather than what is happening outside. Without realising it, we can quickly deny or downplay new and uncomfortable information rather than reshape our worldview to accommodate it; we can convince ourselves that a declining industry will recover when it clearly won't, or that new investment may come through despite the track record in the past.

THE CHALLENGE OF ADJUSTMENT

Data does suggest we stick too much to the status quo and, as a result, are at risk of falling behind. For instance, the biggest survey of attitudes of the British people has a telling finding: we are much more relaxed than the experts are about the impact of technology on jobs; in fact, only 10% of us are very or quite worried about it, whereas the concern amongst economists is much higher.[165]

There is a wide range of ways to make sure we are able to meet new skills needs and adopt new ways of working in our current professions. It would therefore be helpful to clarify that retraining doesn't necessarily need to include a full-blown set of new qualifications, but rather could include things like online research, reading a manual, or remote training.

But research reveals that only 19% of adults are involved in some kind of learning activity,[166] whilst well over half said they haven't completed any studying or training in over three years (or not at all) since leaving education.[167] The latest survey found rates to be the lowest since the survey first began, and there has also been a decline in the number of staff who are being trained to receive a nationally recognised qualification. Furthermore, it is generally people with lower skills levels who are the least likely to retrain.

This is creating a number of challenges across the economy in terms of how demand for new skills is matching supply. To exemplify the problem, we have an "in the middle" issue, by which we mean that our labour market has hollowed out, and even if we alter attitudes and approaches to vocational education, as previously discussed, this problem will still exist because the vast majority of the future workforce are already in employment now. This is a direct result of an insufficient response to rising demand in well-paid skilled jobs and falling demand in mid-level jobs that have typically required the kind of tasks that machines can now complete; for example, administration and secretarial roles, or process and plant and machine operatives.[168]

Having a gap at this level makes us an outlier in many ways,[169] none of which we should be proud of. What we need is a much more efficient distribution of skills to reflect the natural demand for skills and ability in the economy. This is seen to a considerably greater extent in international peers such as France and Germany. And that is clearly what employers want, so there is a mismatch with their demands and signals.

Across a whole swathe of our economy, demand for people to retrain to gain the higher skills that we need is substantially outstripping supply. In advanced manufacturing, for instance, employers are struggling to recruit suitable qualified technicians.[170] There aren't enough people possessing adequate science skills.[171] Key sectors are seriously struggling, where an ageing workforce but a demand for labour for new infrastructure projects – for instance, within the rail industry – is creating a real strain.[172]

This is like an orchestra without woodwind instruments. Or a football team without a midfield. Or yacht racing without the trimmers. You just wouldn't set it up like that. And getting the violinists or the attackers or the helmsman to try and fill in would never work.

This matters a great deal, because we know that

when we leave it too late it can be much harder for the individuals involved. Studies of places like Janesville in the United States show how hard people can find it to adjust when industries are in decline.[173] When those who had worked in the General Motors plant for well over a decade were faced with redundancy, the wider world of work was a mystery to them, and when ex-factory workers arrived at the local college, many couldn't use a computer – and that wasn't just about not being able to use Excel, for example, many didn't even know how to turn one on – and some of them dropped out when they were told they couldn't produce handwritten papers.

Rather than retraining, some workers chose similar roles but far away, in one case commuting 270 miles each way, more than the distance from London to Paris. For those who did retrain, many didn't really know what they were signing up for. Two workers liked cop shows on TV, so they enrolled on a criminal justice programme, graduated top of their class, but then became prison guards at the county jail, which they found to be scary, claustrophobic and badly paid. One of them became so depressed she ended up killing herself. In fact, the suicide rate in Rock County doubled after the General Motors plant closed.

CHANGING WORLD

The evidence is clear that adaptation and flexibility are vitally important, and now more than ever. Why? Because machines are predicted to overtake humans in terms of performing more and more tasks in the workplace,[174] and as more jobs become automated, some roles will be eliminated, whilst completely new ones will emerge.

And this doesn't just apply to jobs in factories. We are more likely to be affected than we might think, even if we thought a machine could never do our job. For instance, city traders will be threatened if machines can manage high frequency market trading; and lawyers will not be immune, as cognitive tasks such as providing legal advice can be automated.

In the jobs that remain, demand for soft skills such as compassion and creativity – uniquely human traits – will increase.[175] For instance, in healthcare a machine can do more of the heavy lifting in terms of tracking patients, but it can't think critically in the same way a human can or provide the compassion needed for effective care.

Other advancements in the workplace will involve more and more global connectivity, more remote working, and changes in how colleagues collaborate together. It's not much of a leap to say that we'll need to be more able to partner with people from different backgrounds and cultures. In response to these trends, the World Economic Forum is clear that "agile learning" is key, so that workers can adapt to "new, previously unimagined futures". The only way we can respond to these technological trends is to be ready to adapt, and stay open to continuous learning. There is also an important role for some transferable skills.[176]

There are other relevant trends, such as greater specialisation by firms in certain tasks which could affect the makeup of employers for each occupation.[177] Internal structures will alter, too, with more freelancers and contractors, and there will be other changes, from an explosion in more data to big shifts in diversity and generational change.

Overall, the life of a learned skill has dropped from 30 years to an average of five years, and the average tenure in a job is four and a half years.[178] Indeed, 90% of CEOs say their company is facing disruptive change, and 70% say their organisation does not yet have the skills required for the future.[179]

It has to be acknowledged, then, that we should all be ready to upskill and adapt to meet the challenges ahead. The international evidence is clear that the extent to which we can reap the rewards of the changing world of work depends critically on the extent to which we can develop new skills in our working careers.[180] This is not a negative thing, as there are clear benefits for us individually, and, collectively, the acquisition of new skills will help drive productivity.

There are a number of things that need to happen to ensure we are ready to meet the skills needs of the future. Some of these are at a macro level, and come down to the incentives and the offers available. Companies have a big role to play, too, not least in setting the culture around training and upskilling. But more importantly, the whole mindset of "learn at school" and "do at work" is outdated now and not fit for the modern world. We simply must keep learning to meet the challenges that lie ahead.

LIFELONG LEARNING

There is no denying that humans are incredible for the most part, and able to adapt to our surroundings and circumstances as we always have. How we go about our lives today would be almost unrecognisable to relatives only a few generations ago. Whole new cities have been built; how we interact with one another has changed immeasurably; what we eat, how we rest, and what entertains us is very different.

Our potential for learning is there and we need to tap into it. One way to help us do that is to change how we think about education and work from the start. The reality these days, and one that we all need to face up to, is that we're much less likely to have a job for life, so a long burst of training for a career which then lasts for decades is becoming far less common. We need to resist the temptation to think that when we leave school, college or university we are done.

Instead, we must think of our working lives more like surfing, and our careers more like a series of waves, and we ride each one for a while. In Newquay, legend has it that the first surfer used a reshaped wooden door as a surfboard. Surfboards have moved on a lot since then, but then so has the world of work, and our attitudes to education need to keep pace. Surfers ride a wave until it falls away, and they know that the Atlantic waters will provide more waves, as it has always done. The changing economy does the same. A career can fall away because what was once in high demand drops in demand; but others become available. Interestingly, 64% of people say they would choose a different career if they could start again.[181]

One of the things that can give us hope is that we have some of the building blocks for this kind of culture. The Workers' Educational Association,[182] established in 1903, was an impressive democratic and voluntary adult education movement. Toynbee Hall began at the end of the 19th century,[183] and to this day continues to provide programmes to improve people's skills.

There are wide benefits to continued learning for society as a whole. As an illustration, go and see The Pitmen Painters, the play by Lee Hall, a truly uplifting story of a group of coalminers who begin evening classes with a master of painting from Kings College, Newcastle, and their paintings go on to take the British art world by storm. The play is based on a true story, and helps illustrate that continuing to learn is good for the health of individuals, including their mental health, and enriches the people and communities around them.

And if further inspiration is needed, there are countless examples of how success can be attributed to acquiring broader skills and exploring different experiences rather than specialising in just one area. It was Steve Jobs's calligraphy experience which gave him the idea of developing fonts and customisable elements for the Mac. Van Gogh was a teacher and a bookseller before becoming a world-famous artist. You might say that these are exceptions, but new research shows that changing path might mean "a period of challenge" at first, but then "usually when people make the leap they improve in all sorts of ways".[184]

LOOKING AHEAD

We are naturally drawn towards maintaining the status quo. There are some advantages to that approach, as it avoids unnecessary risk and makes us feel safe. But this can make us resistant to change, even when change is good for us. In reality, the status quo itself is shifting, and we must, now more than ever, learn to continuously adapt if we are going to thrive in the world of work. The more we embrace that mindset from the start, the easier we will find the whole experience.

Often others can look more objectively at our lives than we can ourselves. Perhaps someone we know and trust has suggested a "mid-life career MOT" based on how the current marketplace is changing? How will we react? Whether we go that far or not upon receiving external advice is entirely up to us; but the challenge can be critical in diagnosing how our skills needs are changing and what we need to do to adapt. Talking things through with others can help us avoid looking at our current situation with the rose-tinted glasses associated with status quo bias: I've always done things this way, and it's always worked out, so I'll continue doing things this way…

We would all benefit from approaching education, right from the outset, as a lifelong thing and a lifetime activity. Many of us might need second and third and fourth changes of direction. That is not a bad thing; rather it is the very best way of dealing with a changing economy and an ever-shifting world of work.

Part Three

THE WIDER WORLD

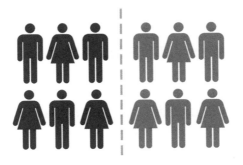

Chapter Seven

FLOCKING TOGETHER

As the benefits become more obvious, the value of integration is understood more clearly. Take children's literature as just one example. It wasn't so long ago that you could read endless children's books and not come across any real diversity. Now there is a much wider range, and we are richer for it.

In *Giraffes Can't Dance*, other animals relentlessly tease Gerald the giraffe about his lanky body; but he soon learns that his confidence and the right music means he can dance without a care in the world. *The Push: A Story of Friendship* follows Marcus and his friend John, who uses a wheelchair, through their many adventures together. *Happy in Our Skin* teaches readers about the beauty of diversity through different families spending time together.

CBeebies is a great example of a real advocate for diversity, with sincere focus on celebrating inclusiveness and kindness. The message of the recent campaign[185] is an inspiring one: children who are friends struggle to spot their differences, showing that children who are exposed to difference early on don't see it the way that we do. Indeed, when asked about what separates them, the answers tend to be things like "living on different roads", "having smaller toes", or the extent to which they like tomato ketchup. And one of its best presenters was awarded an honour for all he did to promote sign language to children.

But while there is fantastic progress to celebrate our differences, there are still major challenges, too. For instance, a recent scene in modern Britain played out as follows: on a rail replacement bus service in Newport, a woman wearing a niqab was chatting to her son in another language. After five minutes, a man suddenly snapped, "If you're in the UK, you should speak English." At this, another passenger turned round and explained, "We're in Wales. And she's speaking Welsh."[186]

More than anywhere else, education should be at the forefront of tackling issues of that kind, and a place where children can breathe the oxygen of diversity and integration and understand why they are so important in modern Britain. Young people are more exposed than ever before to all types of influence, from all parts of the world, and that exposure needs to be accompanied with the skills to navigate it and develop an embracing and positive view of the world.

But according to the OECD,[187] many countries have worrying levels of segregation across their schools and other education institutions, and we are no exception.[188]

IN-GROUPS

The harsh truth is that we all prefer people who are similar to ourselves. If we leave it to freewill, birds of a feather will, in fact, flock together.

Scientists have identified a region of our brains which categorises people as being "like us", even if all we know about them is that they have one thing in common with us.[189]

But the problem with this is, we see them as we see ourselves, rather than form an objective judgement based on more information. Some evidence suggests this even happens amongst infants. When presented with photos on a screen, infants preferred looking at new faces of their own race, unless they had been exposed since birth to people from various races.[190]

Intuitively, it seems, we form "in-groups" and "out-groups", and studies have shown how little encouragement we then need to treat people in a biased way because of the group or category they are in.[191] This is partly explained by our history,[192] because human survival used to be based on group living, and outsiders were seen as very real threats. Of course, that is no longer relevant, and yet it is argued that we still react negatively to groups and their members even when they no longer pose any realistic threat.

It is surprising how easily these groups form. For instance, fans of one sports team can show real loyalty and affection towards one another, and startling aversion towards fans of a rival team when, of course, they are very similar in terms of their basic human qualities, and probably have more in common with each other than with people who don't support a sports team at all!

When it comes to education, this thinking bias applies too, not least because choice is a big driver in determining which education institutions children and young people attend. Indeed, it is possible to go to considerable lengths to get access to a chosen school, even moving to a new area.[193]

But our choice of education institution shapes so much of the early experiences of children and young people and who they meet and interact with. Choice influences the extent to which schools are representative of the local population in terms of different characteristics, such as social class, ethnicity or religion, which in turn has a big impact on contact between communities, exposure to differences, and a whole range of other issues.

WE AND THEY

When we look at the actual choices being made, while there are positives, there is some evidence that the "in-group" bias is at play. As an illustration, the most detailed examination to date of choices of secondary school places shows that parents value academic standards, but this may not actually be the deciding factor.[194] This research shows that one of the most common characteristics that parents value is the social and ethnic composition of a school, but that this isn't always reflected in stated preferences; in other words, this isn't what shows up in survey results. But then we know there can be differences between stated and revealed choices.[195]

Wider research shows that this pattern can hold true in a variety of ways. For example, working-class families may self-exclude from schools with predominantly middle-class student populations, feeling their children might not fit in.[196] They can be more concerned about locality and presence of friends, while middle-class families focus more on school characteristics.[197] And there can be a preference for Muslim schools by aspirant Muslim parents, especially among recent immigrants.[198]

More broadly, research has shown that how people make education choices is systematically related to social class differences,[199] and that in lower social class households the child has a greater role in making the choice.[200] Other systematic differences are linked to knowledge and understanding,[201] which can be lower for new migrants who are less reliant on published information.[202]

In terms of how this all plays out – and of course this is a complex area with many different drivers – various studies have shown that segregation as a result of choice needs to be watched closely.[203] Plenty of literature shows that segregation in schools and other educational settings should not be considered as a topic in isolation, but instead is very closely linked to wider issues around a lack of integration in communities, such as residential segregation.[204] Indeed, they can easily become mutually interdependent and reinforcing.

We know that if we are not careful the consequences of segregation can be serious, and this is true at an individual and a collective level. And there is clear evidence that segregation of children adds to distrust and intolerance of "others".[205] Of concern, too, is how some groups can be pushed to the margins in less well integrated systems, and disengagement from mainstream society can be a risk.[206]

BENEFITS OF DIVERSITY

If we consider the evidence we might well think again before following embedded thinking about in-groups and out-groups. Integration and diversity are not just pleasant things to aim for, they help us navigate the modern world.

There is evidence that children introduced to diversity at a young age develop stronger cognitive skills, such as critical thinking, than those who aren't.[207] And immersing children in cultural diversity gives them more opportunity to become comfortable with the differences they will be exposed to in the wider world.[208] The more diversity becomes the norm early on, the more tolerance and open-mindedness for others grows.

Being able to go on and work with people who are different to us challenges the brain to think in new ways and sharpens up performance. In business, there is evidence to suggest that companies with greater ethnic or gender diversity can make more money.[209] It improves decision-making in other fields, too, such as making law and order fairer. For example, more diverse jury panels made fewer errors during deliberation,[210] and were more aware of potential prejudices. It makes us more innovative as well, and culturally diverse leadership teams are more likely to develop new products, which we will go on to use.[211]

Companies like KPMG, which has worked hard to boost diversity, talk enthusiastically about what they gain from it. The benefits include making full use of all the talent available and fostering an innovative and productive environment. What is more, their view is that the combination of perspectives and experiences is a major factor in driving success.[212]

Society is stronger when the people in it can participate fully and feel a sense of belonging – of being part of a community – in an environment that promotes tolerance and mutual understanding. Where diversity is acknowledged and respected, and minorities are included, societies are more stable and resilient.[213]

One example is the impact of role models and how they can change behaviour. Take the example of Liverpool footballer Mohamed Saleh, a prominent Muslim player. Because of his influence, Merseyside county saw a 18.9% drop in hate crimes, and Liverpool fans halved their rates of posting anti-Muslim tweets.[214] Results show that positive exposure can reveal new information, which changes people's behaviour.

Cohesion empowers people, sustains neighbourhoods and tackles the kind of tensions which could otherwise get out of control: 71% of the 2011 riots in the UK happened in the 10% of areas that most lacked social cohesion.[215] It also improves quality of life and wellbeing.[216]

MORE INTEGRATION

There is hope for the future. There are heartwarming stories of integration all around us, and countless acts of human kindness every day shown to others of all backgrounds. In many ways, we are embracing diversity across the world.

The United States, with its history of slavery and segregation, elected a black president with a Muslim middle name and an African surname. Ireland, a country traditionally famous for its Catholicism, has chosen an openly gay, half-Indian prime minister. In Britain, we pride ourselves on our tolerance and respecting difference, and enjoy watching international films, listening to music from different cultures, and eating food from various corners of the world.

Crucially, we know that education can make a difference. Studies frequently find that contact between different ethnic groups of young people in schools creates more positive attitudes and can increase cohesion. This has been demonstrated directly by examining the positive impact of school mergers in Oldham, and findings included a drop in intergroup anxiety and improvement in attitudes towards other groups.[217]

Through education, we can prepare all young people for life in modern Britain by doing as much as we can to promote integration and diversity. Otherwise, young people could grow up divided, and their earliest experiences will be of groups defined by background or social circumstances: we and they, rather than us. Consequently, they could become more tribal, and could find it harder to live in 21st century Britain.

We can provide further opportunities for inter-action and the building of positive relationships with young people from different backgrounds in a number of ways. For example, when different schools link together there is a positive impact on pupils' skills, attitudes, perception and behaviours.[218] Sporting activities bond young people around a shared activity in which differences do not matter.[219] Other steps have been taken; for instance, Ofsted inspections now encourage educational institutions to promote inclusion.[220] The website Educate Against Hate provides materials which support discussion and reflection on preventing radicalisation and extremism, and encourage children to engage with each other from different perspectives.[221]

The thread that runs through all of these initiatives and programmes is encouraging integration between children and young people from different groups. There is a persuasive argument that information alone is not enough, and we can do more to accelerate the process and closeness of integration through direct contact with each other. Ultimately, we can all play a part, and positively influence a system that is built on differences partly because that is the way our own choices work. When we challenge our own thinking, we build on the hope for much greater integration, with all the benefits of a much stronger society.

We will all be better off if young people develop the skills for life in modern, multicultural Britain, and part of that means being comfortable with diversity and being able to thrive in a diverse and complex world of competing and different views. Education – when we get it right – offers the best opportunities to get that vital preparation.

LOOKING
AHEAD

There is no doubt that the nature of choices like these is particularly complex.[222] But the solution to the issue of in-groups and out-groups is at least partly in our hands, and therefore we can tap into the benefits of greater integration and social cohesion. So how can we set about this challenge?

We can start by recognising that we *all have* a thinking bias which compels us to group together with people "like us". We can acknowledge that our choices apply as much to education as other areas of life, and pause to consider whether we want to underpin our choices in a way that segregates or gathers together.

It might help to keep one eye firmly on the benefits of resisting the in-group bias; on how integration and diversity support young people to prepare for life in the real world, to the stronger wider society they create. Small steps can help at first, such as looking for commonalities with others, putting ourselves in the place of "out-group" members, and reminding ourselves that any differences are normally outweighed by similarities. Ultimately, learning about each other and learning to live and work around each other is in all our interests, both individually and for the long-term productivity and cohesion of our country.

Chapter Eight

WALKING BY

Probably one of the most famous stories about someone going out of their way to help someone else in trouble – and two thousand years after it was written – still has immense relevance today, and it is the parable of the Good Samaritan. A man was travelling from Jerusalem to Jericho and robbers stripped him and beat him and left him half dead. By chance, a priest was going that way, but passed him on the other side of the road, staying away from any danger. Someone else well-placed to help did the same. But then a

Samaritan saw him and, moved by compassion, went to him, bound up his wounds, took him to an inn and paid for him to be taken care of.

The beauty of the story is that the Samaritan is the unlikely hero, although a hated enemy and considered socially inferior at the time. There are other examples of unlikely heroes throughout history, including those who have leapt into action in times of great crisis. From the Second World War there are accounts of remarkable acts of humanity and compassion; for instance, people like Irena Sendler (1910-2008), who was a Polish nurse and is credited with smuggling 2,500 Jewish children out of the Polish capital.[223] Using her brief as a medical officer to carry out sanitary inspections, she would hide children in prams, ambulances and even suitcases. She did so at enormous personal risk and was eventually caught, brutally tortured by her captors, and sentenced to death. But she managed to evade this fate, go on to live to be 98, and tell many people about her story.

We like hearing about stories like that. But are we Good Samaritans ourselves? If we're honest, not always. Perhaps we might recognise some of what Michael Caine meant when he gave his views on being British: "*I think what is British about me is my feelings and awareness of others and their situations. English people are always known to be well mannered and cold, but we are not cold – we don't interfere in your situation. If we are heartbroken, we don't scream in your face with tears – we go home and cry on our own.*"

It seems we are naturally inclined to not show emotion, and be intuitively cautious about what we might consider "interfering". What does it take for us to get involved?

THE BYSTANDER EFFECT

The bystander effect is an interesting study in human behaviour. It happens when the presence of others around us discourages us from intervening in a situation. The term first came about after a murder in New York in 1964. When Kitty Genevose was stabbed to death outside her apartment, a series of neighbours failed to step in to assist her or even call the police (reportedly at the time 38 neighbours were witnesses, although later accounts suggest it was fewer.)[224]

Was this because her neighbours had malicious intentions or were deliberately negligent? No, it was because of "diffused responsibility"; in other words, each neighbour was likely to have thought that someone else would deal with it.

Furthermore, because we take cues from others around us, the neighbours most likely looked at the behaviour of others around them, and no one seemed panicked or especially alarmed, so they felt more reassured – and walked on by.

It is easy to think that we would have acted differently, and hopefully we would have. But we are all inclined to behave in the same way, if we're honest, and this kind of social paralysis has implications for not just what happens on city streets, but also many other aspects of how we work, socialise and live. And it applies not just when there is an emergency, but to every group situation where all it takes is for just *one person* to step forward to do something to help, and the rest will follow. Instead, what happens time and again is that there is a delay while members of the group decide who will be the volunteer to act…and no one acts at all.

While that sounds like a terrible way to live, it makes sense. Acting in difficult or uncomfortable situations is unpleasant. To use a couple of trivial examples, finding the owner whose car alarm is going off might mean going out of our way, and using our precious time and energy, or unblocking a drain that looks like it might cause problems for our surrounding neighbours might make us think, *Why am I doing this? Other people will benefit without putting any effort in*? There is little incentive to act. But in worst-case scenarios, nothing gets done at all and everyone ends up suffering.

More seriously, this unfortunate thinking bias applies to how we react to children and young people, too. How many times have we passed a young person and thought something was wrong, but we didn't want to intervene? How many times have we observed a situation involving a child, and alarm bells have gone off in our heads, but not quite enough to meet our threshold for stepping in?

We get caught between a prompt to act and not wanting to look foolish by jumping to conclusions. Instinctively, we don't want to meddle or pry, and we also don't want to look silly by stepping in only to find that everything is alright, after all, which is why everyone else wisely stayed out of it in the first place. Even young children demonstrate this thinking bias when they are presented with situations in which they could help. For example, one study showed that five-year-olds were less likely to help with tasks such as wiping up a puddle of water in the middle of a room if there were others around who could do so.[225]

BEFORE IT'S TOO LATE

We see bystander effect play out in so many situations. A major survey asked adults in the general public whether people should become involved when they have concerns that a child is being neglected, and 94% agreed we should. But of those who had been very or quite worried about a child, only around two-thirds made a decision to tell someone about their concerns, and only a minority spoke to someone in a professional role.[226] Reasons for not acting included not having sufficient proof or evidence, which suggests that problems need to escalate significantly before many people feel confident enough to take action. This fits wider studies which show there is a mismatch between how people think they will respond and what they actually do in practice.

The reality, though, is that there are many thousands of children in need across the country, not just living in other places or on other streets, but close to each of us, in our own communities. And, sadly, there are rising numbers of cases.[227] Tragically, we know that when warning signs are missed, cases don't go away, instead they can get worse without the right support.

This really matters, because intervention becomes

harder and harder over time. For children and young people, when intervention happens too late, adverse experiences and trauma have both a short-term effect and a long-term impact, even if the immediate risk of harm is resolved.[228] Our resistance for involvement can have far-reaching consequences for the victims, such as disengagement and mental health issues. Unsurprisingly, the impact can affect educational outcomes too,[229] and can lead to other serious issues like social exclusion or unemployment.[230]

The experiences of these children can stay with them throughout their adult lives, even after interventions by social workers and others; and often there can be lasting consequences, such as reduced wellbeing, lower confidence, or difficulty regulating emotions. Traumatised children are increasingly more likely to have behavioural, emotional and social difficulties, too, which we will each need to consider, as these children will go on to be citizens of our society and will live alongside us and interact with us. And, in the more extreme cases, we know there is a link with criminal behaviour.[231] Therefore, helping earlier will help us all as, collectively, whether we like it or not, we are all affected.

We have wonderfully skilled professionals across the country who play a vital role. But if we don't sound the alarm or get involved, given we are talking here about thousands and thousands of young people, some in desperate situations, will we always wonder if we could have done more?

TAKING ACTION

The evidence is clear that bystanders, rather than just being peripheral observers, can make a big difference, and in a wide range of settings. Let's now look at a few different examples that, far from making us look silly, can lead to crucial intervention which otherwise may not have happened.

Bullying is a common problem and, unsurprisingly, those affected enjoy going to school less, have poorer relationships with teachers, and are less likely to feel safe and included. But bullying often isn't tackled. The children don't always come forwards themselves. There can be lots of reasons for that. For the bullied, one is the fear of backlash from others; other reasons include embarrassment, or a perception that no one cares or could understand. However, bystanders are present in the vast majority of bullying situations, and one study shows that more than 50% of the time bullying stops within 10 seconds of a bystander stepping in to help.[232] Consequently, "bystander training" is considered highly effective by school staff who use it.[233] So why, in so many cases, don't we intervene?

Similarly, potential crime could be prevented not by the police, who are highly unlikely to actually witness a crime, but by ordinary citizens going about their day-to-day life who also look out for others.

When it comes to sexual abuse, the frameworks which map how attackers are able to commit this kind of crime show that children will be safer if everyone is educated to spot it and act.[234] This is true not only in terms of safeguarding potential victims, but also that third parties (such as friends or work colleagues) can exert a positive influence over the potential offender so that offences are less likely.[235]

When it comes to child abuse and neglect more generally, we know a great deal now about the key indicators,[236] and evidence shows that there should be clear alarm bells for action: a parent regularly collecting a child from school when drunk; a child with matted hair and consistently poor hygiene; signs of self-harming; overtly sexual or aggressive language or behaviour. If anything like this is seen, we're encouraged to come forward rather than wait until being absolutely certain, which can often mean waiting too long.

Suicide is the biggest killer of young men,[237] and is an issue in some universities. Nearly one in four young people will experience suicidal feelings at least once in their lives, and one in 20 will try and take their own life. Many suicides are preventable,[238] but not necessarily by formal services. In fact, only one in three people who die by suicide are known to mental health services.[239]

Instead, the majority of suicides have been preceded by verbal or behavioural warning signs, and people who kill themselves have often told someone things like they "do not feel life is worth living" or that they "have no future".[240] Acting at the right point can make a huge difference, because heightened suicide risk is often short-term and situation-specific, and while thoughts may be intense, they are not permanent, and they can be addressed.

When it comes to crime, there is clear evidence that even when adolescents have gone as far as engaging in criminal behaviour, this can often be turned around, and many do not continue to commit crimes as adults.[241] The right influence can make a big difference, and the capacity for change is huge, whatever the circumstances or situation, as long as the right support is available.

STEPPING IN

This is where we can *all* make a difference. Anything we notice can be mentioned to the appropriate parties and, consequently, help someone at risk. And if we get involved, we need to ask how we can be useful and do the right things. We could even think in advance about how we might deal with particular situations, like the examples given earlier, so that we are ready. There is excellent advice available online about the roles bystanders can play to tackle the issues raised in this chapter and, without a doubt, there is always something we can do to help in the initial stages.

Of course, in the more complex cases involving vulnerable children and young people, specialist support is required. Much like the message that comes over on the intercom asking, "Is there a doctor on the plane?", some things are best left to the professionals. But this in itself is an interesting example of bystander effect, as in various documented cases, doctors who happened to be on board recalled their surprise that when they got to the patient no one was touching him or her, even though flight attendants are all required to be trained in first aid.

Information is critical, and if we are seriously worried about something we've witnessed there are a number of routes for reporting concerns: our local council, the NSPCC, or the police, for example. We can trust that our concerns will be listened to, and information will be gathered and acted on based on a wealth of professional experience and expertise.

Going beyond that, tackling the issues which affect the children and young people around us is not just a reactive thing, we can help by getting involved *proactively*. More and more there is a collective national effort for each of us to play our part in caring for others. For instance, volunteering at events run by charities like the Children's Society, advocating support for vulnerable young people locally, or supporting groups run for young people. The Boxing Academy in Hackney was set up for the most hard-to-reach young people, and started as a small community project in a boxing gym in Tottenham in 2007. The headteacher got involved because of her experiences with her own adopted son, and it now helps to transform the lives of dozens of excluded and vulnerable young people, saving them from gang culture, knife crime and street violence.[242] As a further example, the lifechanging impact of fostering and adoption is staggering, providing safety and stability when children most need it. And pledges by companies like Barclays and Rolls Royce have been made to set up thousands of work opportunities for care leavers.

Ordinary people can do extraordinary things, and there is lots we can do to help if we resist the urge to just stand by. We hope others would put their heads above the parapet if they spotted things that didn't seem right for somebody we love and care about. We can do the same for them. We can each play a part, big or small.

LOOKING AHEAD

Like so many thinking biases, simply being aware of the bystander effect increases our chances of overcoming it and taking action when called upon to do so. By knowing that our brains will resist us stepping forwards when others around us are staying back, we're more likely to do the right thing and lend a hand in a time of need. This will then encourage others to step forward too, and suddenly we are not on our own.

For us to usefully intervene we need to notice an issue in the first place. A mindset of taking responsibility for the wellbeing of others around us goes a long way, and watching out for children and young people in our community is the starting point. We can then be vigilant for warning signs and spot things which may suggest potential concerns.

We'll be more confident if we know how to respond to various scenarios, such as witnessing bullying, or seeing signs of abuse, or picking up on someone's suicidal thoughts. None of these situations are simple or straightforward, and it's too easy to freeze, making it more likely that we withdraw into bystander mode because we are wired that way. But it is in all our interests that we override this way of thinking. The impact of doing so could be huge.

Conclusion

STEPS TO TAKE

The decisions we make about lots of different things really matter. Take a tennis match, for example. Roger Federer beats other players almost all of the time, partly because of his skill, technique and fitness, but partly because of the choices he makes. Deciding to take a drop shot or coming to the net can be the difference between winning or losing a point, a game, the match. Chess is an even more obvious example. Imagine sitting down to play a grandmaster. Your chess pieces are the same, you play by exactly the same rules, you can see all of the same board...but you will almost certainly lose because he or she will make better decisions than you will.

Even more so, decisions matter when it comes to education, because we are taking a direct role in creating the future – and some things as they happen now are not how they must always be. We can decide what we want in terms of education, the kind of community or world we want to live in, and can set out to make that happen. And thank goodness for that, because we can't wait for automation to take our jobs, mental health issues to consume young people, or segregation to drive our communities apart.

OUR INTUITIONS

As we discussed right at the start, we rely more on intuitive thinking than we might think. The message here is definitely not that we should ignore our intuition, which can play such a useful role, but that with an awareness of thinking biases, and a view of the bigger picture, we can make the best choices. So what should we do with our intuitions when it comes to education?

Intuitive thinking is a powerful thing, and while in

some areas we can develop it through practice and feedback – especially if we are an expert in that field – we don't have much chance to do that when it comes to education. We don't tend to choose schools very often, and there are only so many times we might change career, so solely relying on intuition means we actually might make a bad choice. Far better, then, is the skill to acknowledge the intuition, or subconscious prompt to do with an education choice – and this is true of both good and bad prompts – but then think further, ask others, gather more information, and look at the much bigger picture.

In some ways, this is a bit like spotting fake news, and not in the Donald Trump sense, but rather the meaning that Collins Dictionary gave to this new phrase, when making it Word of the Year in 2017: "False information disseminated under the guise of news reporting." So serious is the issue of fake news that a new charity has been set up in Brussels called Lie Detectors,[243] which sends journalists into schools to explain that we must not believe everything we read, and that we need to verify things we are not sure about. On one level, the aim of the charity is simple: to deal with examples of inaccurate information. For example, they will show children Internet articles saying things like the world's oldest man has turned 179 years old, and then debunk it (it's amazing how many believe it initially!) But the bigger goal is being up front about the failures of modern-day news reporting so that we are all better equipped for life in the 21st century. And right there is the parallel for this book: we can take the opportunity to look at whether our intuition is in fact right, and how it affects our choices, especially when it comes to an area as important as education.

FREEDOM

When it comes to education, we actually have a surprising amount of freedom. To illustrate, let's run through some examples of the amount of choice available to us. There are some niche cases – for example, if a child has never been to school, parents do not need anyone's permission to home educate[244] – but the following are everyday examples, and absolutely central to how education in our country works.

First, there are a wide variety of paths young people can follow, with literally thousands of qualifications that a 16-year-old could take.[245]

Secondly, we have a wide range of education institutions to choose from.

Thirdly, we place a lot of trust in education professionals to make appropriate judgements on the basis that they are best-placed to identify needs. To pick a specific example, it might be of importance to us that children are taught about women in history, but even schools that follow the national curriculum have wide flexibility on this subject.[246] For instance, there is scope for schools to teach pupils about the suffragette movement, or to include information about women as part of black history, and, depending on what a school decides, this could be covered as part of lessons on "the end of Empire" or perhaps "challenges for Britain, Europe and the wider world 1901 to the present day". (Examples of women in history who schools could teach about range from Queen Victoria to Rosa Parks.)

A fourth choice has to do with support and interests outside of formal education, and is very much to do with personal choice. We might decide we want extra tutoring for young people, or allow them to take part in various extra-curricular activities. And how we choose to support children at home, and the environment we create for them to do their homework is essentially up to each of us. Homelife is also subject to a variety of influences, which we need to respond to. There are those which have existed for years; for example, what a child is permitted to watch on TV and for how long. But, as discussed previously, there are new issues to manage now, such as keeping children safe online. This leads to a whole new debate about what is appropriate, and we each must make our own judgements and draw our own conclusions on the use of smart phones, tablets and computers.

COMMON TRAPS

So we each hold power in our hands, and have the freedom to make different decisions about education that shape our lives and the lives of people close to us. This is a great responsibility. It means we all have a role, for better or worse.

There is so much about education in this country which we should celebrate. Much of our education, training and care is top drawer: many good and outstanding schools; a revamped curriculum to keep pace with the best in the world; better understanding than ever before about how to support the most disadvantaged children and help them catch up. Above all, we have wonderful and dedicated professionals. When I spend any time with teachers I am always humbled by their care for the children they work with, and how often they go above and beyond.

But there are still deep issues that are relevant to us all, from growing concern about the use of social media, to frequent worry about whether young people are ready for the modern world, to new waves of redundancies hitting unprepared groups of workers whose skills were only tailored to one industry.

The world is changing, and an interesting point here is that IQs are falling[247] – at least in terms of how we measure them, which means either we are getting less intelligent, or we are no longer able to accurately test intelligence. This could be a cause for great alarm and introspection, or it could just be a sign that we are adapting to the modern world and tests first developed a hundred years ago are no longer that useful to us. Whether that is the case or not, what is apparent is our need to reflect and challenge some of our assumptions.

EMBRACING DIFFERENT CHOICES

This book has covered the top eight areas where the way in which many of us think can be challenged.

In Part 1 we saw that media coverage can present the world as a more negative and dangerous place than it actually is, thus affecting our decisions about risk. We can focus too heavily on single pieces of information, such as class size when making decisions, which can distort our choices. We can downgrade the areas of education that are harder to measure or articulate, especially character education, despite compelling evidence that building good character is as important as achieving good grades.

Part 2 looked at how we might assume that a popular choice by lots of other people must be right for us, but how that can mean we dismiss vocational education, or what might be a better path for us. We also discussed how it is natural to focus on success stories when deciding our career aspirations, but how they are often not representative of what most journeys are actually like. Our attachment to the status quo was included in Part 2, and how we can be slow to adjust to changing circumstances and skills needs if this attachment is too great.

In Part 3 we looked at a different category of thinking bias, in that we are drawn to people like us when making choices about education institutions, but how that can lead to more segregation and less social cohesion. We also saw how we are less likely to intervene and help others around us when the people around us are not helping, but how the result of that is no one steps in until it's too late, even in serious cases of bullying or child abuse, and how this must change if we are to show children and young people that we care, thus paving the way for them to do the same.

These are substantial challenges across the whole of society, and there will never be just one simple solution given the complexity of these issues. Therefore, successful change depends at least in part on each one of us and the choices we make.

OVERCOMING THE BIASES

We can stay open to challenging our thinking. But to do that, awareness of *what* we are thinking and *why* is key.

If we go to Africa on safari, there are amazing wild animals to see: lions, leopards, elephants, rhinos and buffalos. We've all seen them before in books or on TV, and even small children can describe them; but once we have seen them up close, in real life, it is almost impossible to view them in the same way again when we go to the zoo and see them in captivity.

My hope with this book is to achieve something similar, although the setting is somewhat different. We all think we know about a thing, including education. And we've all had intuitive or gut feelings, and we're all prone to thinking biases. But, on closer inspection, up close and in real terms, we just may see them differently once we realise how they affect our choices.

We haven't discussed every aspect of education here, as it is simply too large a subject, but one of the most hotly debated areas – our view of teaching professionals – is no different when it comes to thinking biases. Teachers get paid less than the British public think. Respondents to a survey significantly overestimated the starting secondary school teacher salary.[248] They work harder than most of us would predict, too: over 50 hours a week, on average. Gender stereotyping is another area that deserves our consideration.

Critically, the eight areas outlined in this book represent the most prominent issues with our thinking, and they are the areas where challenging thinking biases has the greatest potential for improving our choices. We hold many of the solutions, at least in part, in our hands, and we are more in control than we might realise. As well as awareness of our thoughts and opinions, the next step is deciding and acting differently to what our biases might be telling us. When we realise our thinking is flawed, we can learn to slow down, assess the facts and information for ourselves as part of the broader view. The reason the Office for National Statistics puts out statistics on violent crime or employment is so that we can understand trends, not just rely on trying to get our heads around the cases we hear about in the press, which will inevitably distort the bigger picture.

There are other things we can do across these eight areas: we can be more open to discussion and debate; we can do more to consider outside views and different perspectives; we can seek out a more balanced view on how apprentice-ships work, or look at the benefits of character development; we can try and understand more about the challenges our vulnerable young people face, such as bullying and depression.

We can also be more open to asking for and accepting help and advice. By being aware of the biases of our thinking and choosing to expand our world view, we are able to design the envi-ronment around us in a way that benefits not just ourselves, but everyone around us.

LOOKING AHEAD

Each chapter of this book has discussed how we can do things differently, if we choose, thus overcoming the most common thinking biases rather than letting them overcome us. In each case, changing the way we think will improve our decision-making.

If I can leave you with one overarching message, it is to trust your ability to challenge these particular thinking biases. If in doubt, slow down and reflect, get more information and advice, and talk potential decisions through with other people.

We live busy lives in a complex world, and bias when it comes to deciding what clothes to wear, or which boxset to watch, is of little consequence in the long term. Education, on the other hand, is decision-making on a whole different level: it is immeasurably important, and lifechanging. Hopefully, consideration of the points in this book will help us to identify and overcome our most prominent biases, so that we are all empowered to think more clearly and make the best education choices.

ACKNOWLEDGEMENTS

My education journey – in a professional sense – began on a September morning in 2007 in front of a year 10 class in north London. I soon realised I had a lot to learn! Rolling forward to today, that is still true. I have been so fortunate since then to have enjoyed a range of invaluable experiences, from teaching amazing young people, to visiting over 100 education institutions, to multiple governor roles, and working as a senior policy adviser in government. I count myself lucky to have worked with so many brilliant people along the way who have profoundly shaped each of those experiences.

The same is true with *The Educated Guess*. While it has been completed purely in a personal capacity, it has been a collaborative effort, and simply would not have happened without the help of dozens and dozens of people. I have been blown away by how generous so many people have been with their time and advice – so thank you a million times over. You know who you are, and I have thanked each of you directly. Thank you, too, to the excellent editors and designers who made this final product possible.

Above all, I owe a big thank you to my family, whose encouragement and backing has been vital. And two particular messages of thanks: firstly, to Dad…you passed away before this book was even an idea; but for someone who left school at 15, you taught me as much about education as anyone else, and this belongs as much to you. And to Anna, my wonderful wife… without you none of this would be possible, and you make everything complete. Thank you for your unwavering and tireless support.

ABOUT THE AUTHOR

Warwick Sharp has over a decade of experience in education policy in a range of senior roles, including senior civil servant in government. Before that, Warwick taught in a secondary school and had responsibility for careers provision. He has been both a school and college governor, and has visited nurseries, schools, colleges and universities up and down the country. Warwick studied economics at Cambridge and has a masters in public policy management. He lives in London with his wife Anna (whose intuitions are always better than his!)

Warwick has always been fascinated by our intuition, and the fast and automatic judgements that we all make. This book combines that with what Warwick considers to be the most important and transformational area of our lives: education. Warwick took a break from government to write this book because he sees it as an opportunity to explore and share some of the main biases in our thinking which come with being human, and how they apply to education. He hopes it is empowering and uplifting, directly useful for us all as we face big education choices, and a catalyst for further material in this important space.

REFERENCES AND ENDNOTES

1   Andy, G. (1990) *Education and State Formation*, Palgrave Macmillan, UK.

2   The first Bill to provide free state education was presented to Parliament by Samuel Whitbread in 1807 but rejected. Objections included that if the poor could read they could be influenced by seditious pamphlets.

3   The Hadow Report, 'Differentiation of the Curriculum for Boys and Girls Respectively in Secondary Schools' (1923), London, HM Stationery Office.

4   Daniel, K. (2012) *Thinking, Fast and Slow*, Penguin.

5   Ibid.

6   The first biases were discovered in the early 1970s, including the seminal work by Kahneman and Tversky (1974) with very wide-ranging evidence ever since.

7   Rozenblit, L., and Keil, F. (2002) 'The misunderstood limits of folk science - the illusion of explanatory depth', Cognitive Science, vol. 26, pp 521-562, at https://cogdevlab.yale.edu/sites/default/files/files/rozenblit%20%26%20keil%20%202002.pdf

8   Oriana, L. 'An Abridged History of Funambulists', Atlas Obscura, 5 November 2014, at https://www.atlasobscura.com/articles/an-abridged-history-of-funambulists

9   Philippe Petit crossed a cable in New York, taking 45 minutes after six years of planning (with no safety net or harness).

10 A televised stunt to walk 550m on two-inch wire.

11 In 1903, Orville Wright piloted the first powered airplane 20 feet above the ground. (The brothers began their experimentation several years earlier following failed attempts by others.)

12 Sir Francis Drake biography at http://www.bbc.co.uk/history/historic_figures/drake_francis.shtml

13 The data scientist Kalev Leetaru applied sentiment mining to The New York Times between 1945 and 2005, and to an archive of translated articles and broadcasts from 130 countries between 1979 and 2010. The news did become more negative over time.

14 First coined by Tversky and Kahneman. See *Judgement under Uncertainty: Heuristics and Biases*, in 1974.

15 Ropeil, D. (2010) *How Risky Is It, Really? Why Our Fears Don't Always Match the Facts', McGraw-Hill Education*, and Chapman, B. (2017) *Shark Attacks: Myths, Misunderstandings and Human Fear*, CSIRO Publishing.

16 Barber, B., Odean, T., and Ning Zhu, (2009) 'Systematic Noise' Journal of Financial Markets, vol. 12, pp 547-569.

17 Klein, J. 'Five pitfalls in decisions about diagnosis and prescribing', British Medical Journal, 31 March 2005, at https://www.bmj.com/content/330/7494/781

18 McMullan, J., and Miller, D. 'Wins, Winning and Winners: The Commercial Advertising of Lottery Gambling', Journal of Gambling Studies, vol. 25, no. 3, pp 273-295, 25 Feb 2009.

19 Department for Transport, 'Walking and Cycling Statistics' updated 30 Aug 2018, at https://www.gov.uk/government/collections/walking-and-cycling-statistics (shows that 44% of all children walked to school).

20 Shaw, B., Watson, B., Frauendienst, B., Redecker, A., Jones,

T., with Hillman, M. (2013) 'Children's independent mobility: a comparative study in England and Germany (1971 to 2010)', Policy Studies Institute at http://www.psi.org.uk/site/publication_detail/852

21 Survey by the National Trust found that children play outside for an average of four hours a week – see https://www.theguardian.com/environment/2016/jul/27/children-spend-only-half-the-time-playing-outside-as-their-parents-did and the Eden Project survey of children in the southwest, which found the average child spends five hours a week playing outside, at https://www.edenproject.com/media/2015/03/traditional-childhood-activities-becoming-a-thing-of-the-past

22 Woolley, H. and Griffin, E. 'Decreasing experiences of home range, outdoor spaces, activities and companions: changes across three generations in Sheffield in north England', Children's Geographies, vol. 13, no. 6, pp 677-691, 2015. This is a small-scale study but reflects findings of a range of other cross-generational research referenced in the report.

23 England Marketing – Report to Natural England, 'Childhood and nature: a survey of changing relationships with nature across generations', 2009. Findings include that over two-thirds of adults were allowed to go alone to play at a friend's house, play in the streets near their homes or in the garden with no supervision, but less than half the children now are allowed to do this.

24 Children's Society, 'Good Childhood Inquiry', 2007. Findings included that 43% of adults thought 14 was earliest age that a child could go out unsupervised. Other findings included that two-thirds of 10-year-olds have never been allowed out alone.

25 Dame Judith Hackitt cited various examples in a speech to the Royal Academy of Engineering in 2016, including that one school told kids they could not wear frilly socks.

26 Association of Teachers and Lecturers survey in 2011, at

https://www.atl.org.uk/Images/18%20April%202011%20-%20Over-zealous%20schools%20ban%20British%20bulldog%20and%20conkers%20-%20ATL.pdf

27 Spielman, A. (2017), at https://www.telegraph.co.uk/news/2017/08/05/children-denied-chance-develop-resilience-strict-health-safety/

28 Spielman, A. (2017) 'Ofsted's Chief Inspector writes about safety culture in schools', at https://www.gov.uk/government/speeches/ofsteds-chief-inspector-writes-about-safety-culture-in-schools

29 'Paparazzi avoidance and self-defence taught to trainee nannies', BBC, 23 Feb 2013, at https://www.bbc.co.uk/news/uk-england-bristol-21598672

30 Survey by The Beano alongside YouGov and Young Minds of 2000 parents of 6-12-year-olds for Safer Internet Day, Jan 2018.

31 Ofcom, 'Children and parents: media use and attitudes report 2018', 29 Jan 2019.

32 Twenge, J. (2018) 'iGen: Why today's super-connected kids are growing up less rebellious, more tolerant, less happy—and completely unprepared for adulthood – and what that means for the rest of us', Atria Books.

33 Office for National Statistics, 'Milestones: journeying into adulthood', 18 Feb 2019, at https://www.ons.gov.uk/peoplepopulationandcommunity/populationandmigration/populationestimates/articles/milestonesjourneyingintoadulthood/2019-02-18

34 Our World in Data is a non-profit website that brings together the data and research on the powerful, long-run trends reshaping our world. See Ourworldindata.org

35 Work by Dr Gregory Rodgers, looking at annual death rates of children under five who accidentally ingested oral prescrip-

tion drugs, showed that death rates dropped by 45% when Govt required drugs to be put in child resistant packages. See 'The effectiveness of child-resistant packaging for aspirin', 2002.

36 Office of National Statistics, 'Being 18 in 2018', 13 Sep 2018, at https://www.ons.gov.uk/peoplepopulationandcommunity/populationandmigration/populationprojections/articles/being18in2018/2018-09-13

37 NSPCC, 'How safe are our children? The most comprehensive overview of child protection in the UK', 2018, at https://learning.nspcc.org.uk/media/1067/how-safe-are-our-children-2018.pdf

38 Department for Transport, 'Facts on Child Casualties', June 2015, at https://assets.publishing.service.gov.uk/government/uploads/system/uploads/attachment_data/file/442236/child-casualties-2013-data.pdf

39 National Water Safety Forum, Water Incident Database – Information, Data and Statistics Annual Drowning Statistics, at https://www.nationalwatersafety.org.uk/news/posts/2019/april/2018-uk-water-related-fatalities-published/

40 Child Accident Prevention Trust, 'Electric Shocks', at https://www.capt.org.uk/electrical-safety

41 Child Accident Prevention Trust, 'Main Causes of Accident and Injury', at https://www.capt.org.uk/pages/category/safety-advice-injury-types

42 National Institute for Health and Care Excellence, 'Physical Activity and children – Review of Learning from Practice: Children and Active Play' (2008) at https://www.nice.org.uk/guidance/ph17/documents/promoting-physical-activity-for-children-consultation-on-the-evidence9

43 See www.clevernevergoes.org (introduced by the charity

Action Against Abduction).

44 Orben, A., Dienlin, T., and Przybylski, A., 'Social media's enduring effect on adolescent life satisfaction', Proceedings of the National Academy of Sciences, 21 May 2019.

45 Sandseter, E., and Kennair, L. (2011) 'Children's Risky Play from an Evolutionary Perspective: The Anti-Phobic Effects of Thrilling Experiences', Evolutionary Psychology.

46 National Institute for children and young people, 'Physical activity for children and young people', 2009, at https://www.nice.org.uk/guidance/ph17

47 Ibid.

48 McCormack, T., O'Connor, E., Beck, S., and Feeney, A., (2016) 'The development of regret and relief about the outcomes of risky decisions', The Journal of Experimental Child Psychology, vol. 148, pp 1-19.

49 LEAP (Learning Early About Peanut allergy) is a randomised controlled clinical trial designed and conducted by the Immune Tolerant Network (ITN) to determine the best strategy to prevent peanut allergy in young children. See www.leapstudy.com

50 Education Endowment Fund, 'Outdoor adventure learning', at https://educationendowmentfoundation.org.uk/evidence-summaries/teaching-learning-toolkit/outdoor-adventure-learning/

51 Sandseter, E. (2011) 'Children's risky play from an evolutionary perspective', Evolutionary Perspective, vol. 9, no.2, pp 257-284.

52 Mahmood, K. (2016) 'Do people overestimate their information literacy skills? A systematic review of empirical evidence on the Dunning-Kruger Effect', Communications in Information Literacy, vol. 10, no. 2, pp 198-213.

53 Poll carried out by Opinion Matters for the Holocaust Memorial Day Trust (HDMT), Jan 2019.

54 UNICEF, 'Children in a digital world', Dec 2017, at https://www.unicef.org/publications/index_101992.html

55 ESRI UK. See the study of 1,000 people in Britain which found that over a third feel that having to keep up with today's "information overload" leaves us stressed-out, anxious and unable to relax. Two-thirds say that the need to keep track of a great deal of information is a "major concern" in their lives.

56 'Why focusing on something helps maintain balance', Science ABC, at https://www.scienceabc.com/sports/why-focussing-on-something-helps-in-maintaining-balance.html

57 Demonstrated through a wide range of studies, such as the work of Kahneman and colleagues (2006), showing that people consistently overestimate the value of money on happiness due to the focusing effect.

58 Schkade, D., and Kahneman, D., (1998) 'Does Living in California Make People Happy? A Focusing Illusion in Judgments of Life Satisfaction', Psychological Science, Vol. 9, No. 5, pp 340–346.

59 Klein, N., and O'Brien, E. (2018) 'People use less information than they think to make up their minds', Proceedings of the National Academy of Sciences, Vol. 115, No. 52, pp 13222-13227, at https://www.pnas.org/content/115/52/13222

60 Montacute, R., and Cullinane, C. (2018) 'Parent Power? How parents use financial and cultural resources to boost their children's chances of success', Sutton Trust at https://www.suttontrust.com/wp-content/uploads/2018/09/Parent-Power-2018.pdf

61 Wespieser, K., Durbin, B., and Sims, D. (2015) 'School choice: the parent view', NFER.

62 TES investigation, 'How do parents pick schools?', TES, 27 May 2016.

63 Montacute, R., and Cullinane, C., (2018) 'Parent Power? How parents use financial and cultural resources to boost their children's chances of success', Sutton Trust at https://www.suttontrust.com/wp-content/uploads/2018/09/Parent-Power-2018.pdf

64 Education Endowment Foundation, 'Class size', at https://educationendowmentfoundation.org.uk/evidence-summaries/teaching-learning-toolkit/reducing-class-size/

65 Education Endowment Foundation, 'Teaching assistants', at https://educationendowmentfoundation.org.uk/evidence-summaries/teaching-learning-toolkit/teaching-assistants/

66 Education Endowment Foundation, 'Mentoring', at https://educationendowmentfoundation.org.uk/evidence-summaries/teaching-learning-toolkit/mentoring/

67 Education Endowment Foundation, 'Built Environment', at https://educationendowmentfoundation.org.uk/evidence-summaries/teaching-learning-toolkit/built-environment/

68 Education Endowment Foundation, 'Digital technology', at https://educationendowmentfoundation.org.uk/evidence-summaries/teaching-learning-toolkit/digital-technology/

69 The Ofsted framework. See https://www.gov.uk/government/publications/education-inspection-framework

70 Department for Education performance tables. See https://www.gov.uk/school-performance-tables

71 Education Endowment Foundation, 'Parental Engagement', at https://educationendowmentfoundation.org.uk/evidence-summaries/teaching-learning-toolkit/parental-engagement/

72 Global Shapers Community, 'The Global Shapers Survey', 2017, at http://shaperssurvey2017.org/

73 'Safe and successful: British explorer completes Antarctic crossing', National Geographic, Dec 2018, at https://www.nationalgeographic.co.uk/travel-and-adventure/2018/12/safe-and-successful-british-explorer-completes-antarctic-crossing

74 Abraham Lincoln, Encyclopaedia Britannica, Updated 12 July 2019, at https://www.britannica.com/biography/Abraham-Lincoln

75 Heath, C., and Tversky, A., (1991) 'Preference and Belief: ambiguity and competence in choice under uncertainty', Journal of Risk and Uncertainty, vol.4, no.1, pp 5-28.

76 Berkowitz, M. (2002) 'The Science of Character Education', Bringing in a new era in character education, vol. 508, pp 43-63.

77 Sockett, H., and Le Page, P., (2002) 'The missing language of the classroom', Teaching and Teacher Education, Vol 18, pp 159-171.

78 Berkowitz, M. (2002) 'The Science of Character Education', Bringing in a new era in character education, vol. 508, pp 43-63.

79 Biesta, G. (2010) 'Why 'What Works' Still Won't Work: From Evidence-Based Education to Value-Based Education', Studies in Philosophy and Education, vol 29, no. 5, pp 491-503.

80 Department for Education, 'Developing character skills in schools', 2017, at https://www.gov.uk/government/publications/developing-character-skills-in-schools

81 Parentkind, 'Children's Mental Health and Wellbeing – Findings from the 2018 Annual Parents Survey', at https://www.parentkind.org.uk/Research--Policy/Research/Annual-Parent-Survey-2018

82 Jubilee Centre for Character and Virtues, 'Character Education in UK Schools – Research Report', 2015, at https://www.jubileecentre.ac.uk/1557/projects/research-reports/character-education-in-uk-schools

83 'Parents more concerned about results than child's happiness, says survey', at https://www.theguardian.com/education/2016/sep/02/parents-concerned-about-results-than-childs-happiness-says-survey

84 Jubilee Centre for Character and Virtues, ' A Framework for Character Education in Schools', 2017, at https://www.jubileecentre.ac.uk/userfiles/jubileecentre/pdf/character-education/Framework%20for%20Character%20Education.pdf

85 Morrison Gutman, L., and Vorhaus, J. 'The Impact of Pupil Behaviour and Wellbeing on Educational Outcomes', Institute of Education, University of London, Childhood Wellbeing Research Centre, at https://assets.publishing.service.gov.uk/government/uploads/system/uploads/attachment_data/file/219638/DFE-RR253.pdf

86 Education and Endowment Foundation, 'Character and Essential Life Skills', at https://educationendowmentfoundation.org.uk/school-themes/character/

87 Sandoval-Hernandez, A., and Cortes, D. (2012) 'Factors and conditions that promote academic resilience: a cross-country perspective'.

88 See Content.time.com including references to straight moral sense and how his instincts were an ideal political model.

89 Romero, L. '5 unexpected entrepreneurship lessons from albert Einstein', Forbes, 26 July 2017, at https://www.forbes.com/sites/luisromero/2017/07/26/5-unexpected-entrepreneurship-lessons-from-albert-einstein/#574be1a51756

90 Report by Edge Foundation (29 Nov 2018) shows that over half of employers value broader skills such as problem solving; 75% of employers say they value employability skills – communication skills, creativity, problem solving, resilience – as much as qualifications.

91 Gutman, L., and Schoon, I. 'The impact of non-cognitive skills on outcomes for young people – literature review', Institute of Education, 21 Nov 2013.

92 Prevoo, T., and Bas ter Weel, (2013) 'The Importance of Early Conscientiousness for Socio Economic Outcomes: evidence from the British cohort study', Institute for the Study of Labor, Discussion Paper No. 7537 at http://ftp.iza.org/dp7537.pdf

93 Moffitt, T., et al (2011) 'A gradient of childhood self-control predicts health, wealth, and public safety', Proceedings of the National Academy of Sciences of the United States of America, Vol. 108, No. 7, pp 2693-2698.

94 Duckworth, D. (2016) 'Grit: Power of Passion and Perseverance', Schribner Book Company.

95 Jubilee Centre for Character and Virtues, ' A Framework for Character Education in Schools 2017 at https://www.jubileecentre.ac.uk/userfiles/jubileecentre/pdf/character-education/Framework%20for%20Character%20Education.pdf

96 Office of National Statistics, 'Children's and young people's experiences of loneliness: 2018', Dec 2018, at https://www.ons.gov.uk/peoplepopulationandcommunity/wellbeing/articles/childrensandyoungpeoplesexperiencesofloneliness/2018

97 'Concerns over children's mental health services', 21 Nov 2018, at https://www.itv.com/news/2018-11-21/concerns-over-childrens-mental-health-services/

98 Office of National Statistics, 'Young people's well-being:

2017', 13 April 2017, at https://www.ons.gov.uk/releases/young-peopleswellbeing2017

99 University of East Anglia introducing dog walking and Teesside university giving colouring books and pens. See The Times on 12 Jan 2019, 'Stressed out students told to take dogs for campus walks', at https://www.thetimes.co.uk/edition/news/stressed-out-students-told-to-take-dogs-for-campus-walks-2dq55ssqk

100 London Economics, 'National Citizenship Service 2010 Evaluation – Main report', Dec 2017, at https://assets.publishing.service.gov.uk/government/uploads/system/uploads/attachment_data/file/678057/NCS_2016_EvaluationReport_FINAL.pdf

101 Institute for Social Innovation and Impact at the University of Northampton, 'Social Impact resulting from the expenditure on cadets', at https://www.northampton.ac.uk/research/research-institutes/institute-for-social-innovation-and-impact/social-impact-resulting-from-expenditure-on-cadets/

102 Culliane, C., and Montacute, R., (2017) 'Life lessons, Improving essential life skills for young people', Sutton Trust.

103 Ofsted, 'Going the extra mile, Ofsted, Excellence in competitive school sport', 20 June 2014, at https://www.gov.uk/government/publications/going-the-extra-mile-excellence-in-competitive-school-sport

104 Department for Education, 'My Activity Passport – editable activity checklist', 28 Dec 2018, at https://www.gov.uk/government/publications/my-activity-passport

105 By the Jubilee Centre for Character and Virtues.

106 Weightman, G. (2010) 'The Industrial Revolutionaries: The Making of the Modern World 1776-1914', Grove Press.

107 Allen, R. (2009) The British Industrial Revolution in Global Perspective', Cambridge University Press.

108 'James Watt', at https://www.famousscientists.org/james-watt/

109 'Isambard Kingdom Brunel 1806-1859', at https://www.networkrail.co.uk/who-we-are/our-history/eminent-engineers/isambard-kingdom-brunel-1806-1859/

110 'Sir Richard Arkwright 1732-1792', at http://www.bbc.co.uk/history/historic_figures/arkwright_richard.shtml

111 House of Commons Library, 'A short history of apprenticeships in England: from medieval craft guilds to the twenty-first century', 9 March 2015, at https://commonslibrary.parliament.uk/economy-business/work-incomes/a-short-history-of-apprenticeships-in-england-from-medieval-craft-guilds-to-the-twenty-first-century/

112 The bandwagon effect is a psychological phenomenon whereby people do something primarily because other people are doing it, regardless of their own beliefs, which they may ignore or override. The origin of the phrase comes from the use of a bandwagon, which is a float in a parade that encourages people to jump aboard and enjoy the music that is being played.

113 A study covering the 1992 US Presidential Election showed that students who learned that Bill Clinton was leading the race in some polls switched their intended vote from Bush to Clinton. See also Richard Nadeau, Edouard Cloutier, and JH Guay, 'New Evidence About the Existence of a Bandwagon Effect in the Opinion Formation Process', International Political Science Review, vol. 14, no. 2, pp 203-213.

114 Office of National Statistics, 'How has the student population changed?', Sept 2016, at https://www.ons.gov.uk/peoplepopulationandcommunity/birthsdeathsandmarriages/livebirths/

articles/howhasthestudentpopulationchanged/2016-09-20

115 Sellgren, K. 'England university applications hit record numbers', BBC, 11 July 2019, at https://www.bbc.co.uk/news/education-48937821

116 NFER, 'Changing attitudes to vocational education', Nov 2014, at https://nfer.ac.uk/media/2323/99947.pdf

117 Kettlewell, K., McCrone, T., and Straw, S. 'Perceptions of higher education and higher and degree apprenticeships', NFER, 2 July 2019, at https://www.nfer.ac.uk/perceptions-of-higher-education-and-higher-and-degree-apprenticeships/

118 Teacher Toolkit, 'Raising the Profile of Apprenticeships', 8 July 2019, at https://www.teachertoolkit.co.uk/2019/07/08/apprenticeships/

119 Forest, M. (2003) 'The Abolition of Compulsory Latin and its Consequences', pp 42-66 in The Classical Association: the First Century 1903-2003, Oxford University Press.

120 Michelle Obama speech to Elizabeth Garrett Anderson school in Islington, London on April 2, 2009.

121 Department for Education, 'Undergraduate degrees: labour market returns', 27 Nov 2018, at https://www.gov.uk/government/publications/undergraduate-degrees-labour-market-returns

122 See 'UCAS postgraduate entry requirements', at https://www.ucas.com/postgraduate/choosing-course/ucas-postgraduate-entry-requirements

123 Universities UK, 'International Students now worth £25 billion to UK economy – new research', 6 March 2017, at https://www.universitiesuk.ac.uk/news/Pages/International-students-now-worth-25-billion-to-UK-economy---new-research.aspx

124 Coughlan, S. 'In fact one in seven countries has a leader who studied in the UK', BBC, 25 Sept 2014, at https://www.bbc.com/news/education-29361704

125 'UCL Urban Laboratory launches university-led urban regeneration case studies', 29 Sept 2015, at https://www.ucl.ac.uk/urban-lab/news/2015/sep/ucl-urban-laboratory-launches-university-led-urban-regeneration-case-studies

126 Collini, S. (2002) *What Are Universities For*?, Penguin.

127 Office of National Statistics, 'One in three graduates over-educated for their current role', 29 April 2019, at https://www.ons.gov.uk/news/news/oneinthreegraduatesovereducatedfortheircurrentrole

128 Office of National Statistics, 'Personal and economic well-being in the UK: April 2019', 11 April 2019, at https://www.ons.gov.uk/peoplepopulationandcommunity/wellbeing/bulletins/personalandeconomicwellbeingintheuk/april2019. See also Dolan, P., Peasgood, T., and White, M. (2008) 'Do we really know what makes us happy? A review of the economic literature associated with subjective wellbeing', Journal of Economic Psychology, vol. 29, pp 94-122.

129 Plackle, I., et al (2014) 'Students preferred characteristics of learning environments in vocational secondary education', International Journal for Research in Vocational Education and Training, vol. 1, pp107-124.

130 Simmons, J. (2014) 'The nature of knowledge in the higher vocational curriculum', Lea J. (ed), Supporting Higher Education in College Settings, London, SEDA.

131 Commission of Adult Vocational Teaching and Learning, 'It's about work... Excellent Adult Vocational Teaching and Learning', 25 March 2013.

132 NFER, 'A literature review of the value of vocational qualifications – a final report', June 2015, at https://www.nfer.ac.uk/media/1910/jcqr01.pdf

133 Institute for Apprenticeships and Technical Education occupational maps. See https://www.instituteforapprenticeships.org/about/occupational-maps/. The maps document all the skilled occupations that can be achieved through an apprenticeship or T Level qualification. Occupations are grouped together to show linkages between them and possible routes for progression.

134 Report of the Independent Panel on Technical Education, April 2016, at https://assets.publishing.service.gov.uk/government/uploads/system/uploads/attachment_data/file/536046/Report_of_the_Independent_Panel_on_Technical_Education.pdf. See in particular Table 3 and the estimate of over 13 million people employed in occupations within technical routes.

135 The Further Education Funding Council, 'Post 16 vocational education and training in Denmark – International report', May 1994, at https://dera.ioe.ac.uk/3430/1/post_16_-_denmark.pdf

136 Report of the Independent Panel on Technical Education, April 2016, at https://assets.publishing.service.gov.uk/government/uploads/system/uploads/attachment_data/file/536046/Report_of_the_Independent_Panel_on_Technical_Education.pdf.

137 Ibid. See in particular Annex C: International Annex.

138 The Bryce Report (1895), 'Report of the Royal Commission on Secondary Education', HM Stationery Office, at http://www.educationengland.org.uk/documents/bryce1895/bryce1895.html

139 Wilkinson, R., and Pickett, K. (2010) *The Spirit level: Why Equality Is Better For Everyone*, Penguin.

140   Plomin, R., and von Stumm, S. (2018) 'The new genetics of intelligence', Nature Reviews Genetics, vol. 19. pp. 148-159.

141   Wald, A. (1943) 'A Method of Estimating Plane Vulnerability Based on Damage of Survivors', Statistical Research Group, Columbia University.

142   Nati, M. 'The world's oldest living people share how they've managed to live so long', at https://www.ranker.com/list/aging-tips-from-worlds-oldest-people/michelle-nati

143   Messi, L. "You have to fight to reach your dream. You have to sacrifice and work hard for it."

144   City and Guilds, 'Great Expectations Research', Nov 2015, at   https://www.cityandguilds.com/-/media/cityandguilds-site/documents/apprenticeships/archive/emsi-reports/cggreatex-pectationsonline-pdf.ashx

See also Office of National Statistics, 'Young people's career aspirations versus reality', Sept 2018, at https://www.ons.gov.uk/employmentandlabourmarket/peopleinwork/employmentandemployeetypes/articles/youngpeoplescareeraspirationsversus-reality/2018-09-27

145   Mann, A., Massey, D., Glover, P., Kashefpadkel, E., and Dawkins, J. 'Nothing in Common: the career aspirations of young Britons mapped against projected labour market demand (2010-2020)', UKCES and Education and Employers, March 2013.

146   Phelps, M. (2008) *No Limits: The Will to Succeed*, Simon and Schuster.

147   Siebert, V. 'Michael Phelps: The Man who was built to be a swimmer', 25 April 2014, at https://www.telegraph.co.uk/sport/olympics/swimming/10768083/Michael-Phelps-The-man-who-was-built-to-be-a-swimmer.html

148   O'Reilly, J. 'Rich List 2019: Why failing exams is no bar to

financial success', The Sunday Times, 12 May 2019, at https://
www.thetimes.co.uk/article/why-failure-at-school-is-no-bar-to-
financial-success-sunday-times-rich-list-67cxq0bsk

149 Coughlan, S. 'Are billionaires more likely to be graduates?',
BBC, 24 Feb 2016, at https://www.bbc.co.uk/news/business-
35631029

150 'Arnold Schwarzenegger', at https://www.evolutionof-
bodybuilding.net/arnold-schwarzenegger/

151 Boston Consulting Group and Sutton Trust, 'The State of
Social Mobility in the UK', July 2017.

152 Institute for Fiscal Studies, 'The relative labour market
returns to different degrees – Research Report', June 2018, at
https://assets.publishing.service.gov.uk/government/uploads/
system/uploads/attachment_data/file/714517/The_relative_
labour_market-returns_to_different_degrees.pdf

153 Office of National Statistics, 'Young people's career aspirations versus reality', Sept 2018, at https://www.ons.gov.uk/
employmentandlabourmarket/peopleinwork/employmentan-
demployeetypes/articles/youngpeoplescareeraspirationsversus-
reality/2018-09-27

154 Mann, A., Massey, D., Glover, P., Kashefpadkel, E., and
Dawkins, J. (2013) 'Nothing in Common: the career aspirations of
young Britons mapped against projected labour market demand
(2010-2020)', UKCES and Education and Employers.

155 Dweck, C. (2017) *Mindset – Changing the way you think to
fulfil your potential*, Robinson.

156 'Good Career Guidance', at https://www.gatsby.org.uk/
education/focus-areas/good-career-guidance

157 The Careers & Enterprise Company was established in
2015 to help link schools and colleges to employers in order

to increase employer engagement for young people. See www.careersandenterprise.co.uk

158 Chambers, N. 'Jobs of the Future: How do young people's career aspirations compare to projected workforce demands?', 14 June 2019, at https://www.oecd-forum.org/users/264950-nick-chambers/posts/50031-jobs-of-the-future-how-do-young-people-s-career-aspirations-compare-to-projected-workforce-demands

159 Crafts, N. 'British Economic Growth in the Steam Age: Some Lessons for Today', University of Warwick.

160 Bessen, J. (2015) 'Learning by Doing: The Real Connection between Innovation, Wages and Wealth', Yale University Press.

161 Thompson, F. (1989) 'The Rise of Respectable Society; Harvard University Press.

162 Zeckhauser, R., and Samuelson, W. (1988) 'Status Quo Bias in Decision Making', Journal of Risk and Uncertainty, Vol. 1, No. 1, pp 7-59.

163 Ibid.

164 Ibid.

165 Natcen, 'British Social Attitudes 35', 2018 edition.

166 Department for Education, 'Adult Participation in Learning Study 2017', 22 Aug 2018, at https://www.gov.uk/government/publications/adult-participation-in-learning-survey-2017

167 Ibid.

168 According to research at Oxford University by Chris Holmes at the Oxford University Centre on 'Skills, Knowledge and Organizational Performance', for every ten middling skilled jobs that disappeared between 1996 and 2008 about 4.5 were high skill and about 5.5 were low skill.

169 Field, S. (2018) 'The missing middle: higher technical education in England', Gatsby, at http://www.gatsby.org.uk/uploads/education/the-missing-middle-higher-technical-education-in-england.pdf

170 Lord Economic Affairs Committee, 'Treating students fairly, the economics of post-school education', House of Lords, 11 June 2018, at https://publications.parliament.uk/pa/ld201719/ldselect/ldeconaf/139/139.pdf

171 House of Commons Committee of Public Accounts, 'Delivering stem skills for the economy', 13 June 2018, at https://publications.parliament.uk/pa/cm201719/cmselect/cmpubacc/691/691.pdf

172 NSARE, 'Forecasting the skills challenge', 2013.

173 Goldstein, A. (2017) *Janesville: An American Story*, Simon and Schuster.

174 World Economic Forum, 'The Future of Jobs Report 2018', 2018, at http://www3.weforum.org/docs/WEF_Future_of_Jobs_2018.pdf

175 Ibid.

176 OECD, 'The Future of Work', at http://www.oecd.org/els/emp/future-of-work/data/

177 The Alan Turing Institute report. 'Understanding the changing world of work', at https://www.turing.ac.uk/research/research-projects/understanding-changing-world-work

178 2017 Deloitte Global Human Capital Trends, and see Graatton and Scott, *The 100 year life: Living and Working in an Age of Longevity* (2016), Bloomsbury, and Thomas and Seely Brown, *A New Culture of Learning: Cultivating the Imagination for a World of Constant Change* (2011), CreateSpace.

179   Deloitte Insights, 'Aligning the organisation for its digital future – Findings from the 2016 digital business global executive study and research report 2016', 25 July 2016, at https://www2.deloitte.com/insights/us/en/topics/emerging-technologies/mit-smr-deloitte-digital-transformation-strategy.html

180   OECD, 'Future ready adult learning systems – United Kingdom', Feb 2019, at http://www.oecd.org/unitedkingdom/Future-ready-adult-learning-2019-United-Kindgom.pdf.   And OECD, 'The Future of Work', at http://www.oecd.org/els/emp/future-of-work/data/

181   Survey by Censuswide, on behalf of Get into Teaching, Nov 2018.

182   See www.wea.org.uk

183   Bynner, J. 'Whatever happened to lifelong learning? And does it matter?' UCL Institute of Education, 14 Sep 2016.

184   'Don't tell me the score', Interview with David Epstein, BBC Radio 4, 18 July 2019.

185   Campaign, 'Everyone's welcome', at https://www.bbc.co.uk/cbeebies/grownups/everyones-welcome

186   Bradbury, T. 'Welsh Woman on bus shuts down racist who told a Muslim passenger to "speak English"', BBC Newsbeat, 21 June 2016, at http://www.bbc.co.uk/newsbeat/article/36580448/welsh-woman-on-bus-shuts-down-racist-who-told-muslim-passenger-to-speak-english

187   Organisation of Economic Cooperation and Development – an international organisation representing over 30 developed countries.

188   See for example Richard Garner, 'UK schools the most socially segregated in the world', Independent, 11 Sept 2012, at https://www.independent.co.uk/news/education/educa-

tion-news/uk-schools-the-most-socially-segregated-in-the-world-8125908.html drawing on figures in the annual review of international education standards published by the Organisation for Economic Co-operation and Development which show that for instance 80% of migrants' children are clustered in disadvantaged schools with fellow migrant pupils. Only three of the 34 countries in the OECD have a worse record – Mexico, Estonia and Finland. But note that other OECD studies have painted a more positive picture, including PISA 2015.

189   Jenkins, A., and Mitchell, J. (2011) 'Medial prefrontal cortex subserves diverse forms of self-reflection', Social Neuroscience, vol. 6, no. 3, pp 211-218.

190   Bar-Haim, Y., Ziv, T., Lamy, D., and Hodes, R. 'Nature and Nurture in Own-Race Face Processing', Psychological Science, Vol. 17, No.2, pp 159-163, 1 Feb 2006.

191   See the minimum group paradigm study, experiments by Henri Tajfel and colleagues.

192   Neuberg, S., and Cottrell, C. (2008) 'Managing the Threats and Opportunities afforded by Human Sociality', Group Dynamics Theory Research and Practice, vol. 12, no. 1, pp 63-72.

193   Montacute, R., and Cullinane, C. 'Parent Power? How parents use financial and cultural resources to boost their children's chances of success', Sutton Trust, Sept 2018, at https://www.suttontrust.com/wp-content/uploads/2018/09/Parent-Power-2018.pdf

194   Burgess, S., Greaves, E., Vignoles, A. 'School Choice in England: evidence from national administrative data', Oxford Review of Education, 22 May 2019.

195   Chakrabarti, R., and Roy, J. (2007) 'Economics of Parental Choice', International Encyclopedia of Education. See also Brian Jacob and Lars Lefgren, 'What do parents value in education?

An empirical investigation of parents' revealed preferences for teachers', The Quarterly Journal of Economics, vol. 122, no. 4, pp 1603–1637.

196 Reay, D., and Ball, S. (1997) 'Spoilt for Choice: The Working Classes and Educational Markets', Oxford Review of Education, vol. 23, no. 1, pp 89-101.

197 Ray, D., and Ball, S. (2013) 'Making their minds up: Family Dynamics of School Choice', British Educational Research Journal, vol, 24, no. 4, pp 431-448.

198 Weekes-Bernard, D. (2007) 'School Choice and ethnic segregation – educational decision-making among black and minority ethnic parents', The Runnymede Trust.

199 Ball, S., Bowe, R., and Gerwitz, S. (1996) 'School choice, social class and distinction: the realization of social advantage in education', Journal of Education Policy, Vol. 11, No. 1, pp 89-112.

200 Reay, D., and Ball, S. (1998) 'Making their minds up: Family Dynamics of school choice', British Educational Research Journal, Vol. 24, No. 4, pp 431-448.

201 Bryne, B., and De Tona, C. (2012) 'Trying to find the extra choices: Migrant families and secondary school choice in Greater Manchester', British Journal of Sociology of Education, Vol. 33, No. 1, pp 21-39.

202 Ball, S., and Vincent, C. (1998) 'I heard it on the grapevine: hot knowledge and school choice', British Journal of Sociology of Education, Vol. 19, No.3, pp 377-400.

203 Windle, J. (2015) 'Making Sense of School Choice: Politics, Policies and Practice under Conditions of Cultural Diversity', Palgrave Macmillan, US.

204 McArdle, N., and Acevedo-Garcia, D. 'Consequences of

Segregation for Children's Opportunity and Wellbeing', Joint Center for Housing Studies, Harvard University, 20 Nov 2017.

205   Ibid.

206   Home Office, 'Radicalisation - the counter-narrative and identifying the tipping point, government response', 18 Dec 2017, at https://www.gov.uk/government/publications/radicalisation-the-counter-narrative-and-identifying-the-tipping-point-government-response

207   Stuart Wells, A., Fox, L., and Cordova-Cobo, D. 'How racially diverse schools and classrooms can benefit all students', The Century Foundation, 9 Feb 2016, at https://tcf.org/content/report/how-racially-diverse-schools-and-classrooms-can-benefit-all-students/?agreed=1

208   Ibid.

209   Rock, D., and Grant, H. 'Why Diverse Teams are Smarter', Harvard Business review, 4 Nov 2016, at https://hbr.org/2016/11/why-diverse-teams-are-smarter. And McKinsey and Co examined over 1000 companies across 12 countries in 2015. See Hunt, V., Yee, L Prince, S., and Dixon-Fyle, S. 'Delivering Through Diversity', McKinsey, Jan 2018, at https://www.mckinsey.com/business-functions/organization/our-insights/delivering-through-diversity

210   Sommers, S. (2006) 'On racial diversity and group decision making: Identifying Multiple Effects of Racial Composition on Jury Deliberations', Journal of Personality and Social Psychology, vol. 90, No. 4, pp 597–612.

211   Lee, N., and Nathan, M. (2013) 'Does Cultural Diversity Help Innovation in Cities: Evidence from London Firms', Economic Geography.

212   KMPG, 'Inclusion, Diversity and Social Equality' at https://

home.kpmg/uk/en/home/about/people/inclusion-diversity.html

213   Labadi, S. (2013) 'Culture: a driver and enabler of social cohesion' in: UNESCO International Congress 'Culture: Key to Sustainable Development', UNESCO.

214   Alrababa'h, A., Marble, W., Mousa, S., and Siegel, A. 'Can Exposure to Celebrities reduce prejudice? The Effect of Mohamed Saleh on Islamophobic Behaviours and Attitudes', 31 May 2019.

215   Experian analysis cited in '5 days in August – an interim report on the 2011 English riots', Riots Communities and Victims Panel, 28 Nov 2011.

216   Delhey, J., Dragalov, G., Boehnke, K. 'Social cohesion and wellbeing in Europe' Eurofound, 12 Nov 2018, at https://www.eurofound.europa.eu/publications/report/2018/social-cohesion-and-well-being-in-europe

217   Department for Education, 'Diversity and Social Cohesion in Mixed and Segregated Secondary Schools in Oldham', 1 Aug 2017, at https://www.gov.uk/government/publications/diversity-and-social-cohesion-in-oldham-secondary-schools

218   Kerr, D., Keating, A., Poet, H., Spielhofer, T., Lopes, J., and Mundy, E. 'Evaluation of the Schools Linking Programme', NFER, March 2011, at https://assets.publishing.service.gov.uk/government/uploads/system/uploads/attachment_data/file/192999/DFE-RB090.pdf

219   Department for Digital, Culture, Media and Sport, 'A review of the social impacts of culture and sport', 25 March 2015, at https://www.gov.uk/government/publications/a-review-of-the-social-impacts-of-culture-and-sport

220   Ofsted inspectors will look for the extent to which the provider prepares learners for life in modern Britain by:

– equipping them to be responsible, respectful, active citizens who contribute positively to society;

– developing their understanding of fundamental British values;

– developing their understanding and appreciation of diversity;

– celebrating what we have in common and promoting respect for the different protected characteristics as defined in law.

See https://assets.publishing.service.gov.uk/government/uploads/system/uploads/attachment_data/file/801429/Education_inspection_framework.pdf

221 See www.educateagainsthate.com. This website gives teachers, parents and school leaders practical advice and information on protecting children from extremism and radicalisation.

222 Manzoni, C., and Rolfe, H. 'Promoting ethnic and religious integration in schools: a review of evidence', National Institute of Economic and Social Research, April 2019, at https://www.niesr.ac.uk/sites/default/files/publications/NIESR%20DfE%20final%20report.pdf

223 Summerlad, J. 'Three unsung heroes who helped Europe's Jews escape the Nazis', The Independent, 27 Jan 2019, at https://www.independent.co.uk/news/world/europe/holocaust-memorial-day-2019-war-heroes-saved-jews-nazis-irena-sendler-frank-foley-raoul-wallenberg-a8745626.html

224 Latane, B., and Darley, J. (1968) 'Bystander intervention in emergencies: Diffusion of responsibility', Journal of Personality and Social Psychology, vol. 8, no. 4, pp 377-383.

225 Plotner, M., Over, H., Carpenter, M., and Tomasello, M. (2015) 'Young children show the bystander effect in helping situations', vol. 26, no. 4, pp 499-506.

226 Burgess, C., Daniel, B., Scott, J., Dobbin, H., Mulley,

K., and Whitfield, E. 'Preventing child neglect in the UK: What makes services accessible to children and families? An annual review', Action for Children in partnership with the University of Sterling, March 2014, at https://www.actionforchildren.org.uk/media/3214/preventing-child-neglect-in-the-uk annual-review march2014.pdf

227 Department for Education, 'Statistics: children in need and child protection', 25 Oct 2018, at https://www.gov.uk/government/collections/statistics-children-in-need

228 The Children's Society, 'Trauma and Young People, A guide for parents, carers and professionals', Oct 2017, at https://www.childrenssociety.org.uk/what-we-do/resources-and-publications/trauma-and-young-people-a-guide-for-parents-carers-and

229 Department for Education, 'Children in need of help and protection – Data and analysis', 16 March 2018, at https://www.gov.uk/government/publications/children-in-need-of-help-and-protection-data-and-analysis

230 House of Commons Committee of Public Accounts, 'Care leavers' transition to adulthood, Fifth Report of Session 2015-16', Oct 2015, at https://publications.parliament.uk/pa/cm201516/cmselect/cmpubacc/411/411.pdf

231 Ministry of Justice, 'Prisoners' childhood and family backgrounds', 11 Feb 2014, at https://www.gov.uk/government/publications/prisoners-childhood-and-family-backgrounds (showing that almost a quarter of the adult prison population and almost half of young men under 21 years old in the criminal justice system have spent time in care).

232 Craig, W., and Pepler, D. 'Observations of bullying and victimisation in the school yard', Canadian Journal of School Psychology, vol. 13, no. 2, pp 41-60, 1 June 1998.

233 Thompson, F., and Smith, P. 'The use and effectiveness

of anti-bullying strategies in schools', Goldsmiths College, April 2011, at https://assets.publishing.service.gov.uk/government/uploads/system/uploads/attachment_data/file/182421/DFE-RR098.pdf

234 Smallbone, S., Marshall, W., and Wortley, R. (2008) 'Preventing Child Sexual Abuse: Evidence, Policy and Practice'.

235 Eck, J., and Madensen, T., (2010) 'Places and the Crime Triangle', Encyclopedia of Criminological Theory.

236 Department for Education, 'Together we can tackle child abuse', at https://tacklechildabuse.campaign.gov.uk/

237 Campaign Against Living Miserably, 'Suicide', at https://www.thecalmzone.net/help/get-help/suicide/

238 World Health Organisation, 'Preventing Suicide: a global imperative', at https://www.who.int/mental_health/suicide-prevention/world_report_2014/en/

239 Universities UK, 'Suicide Safer Universities', at https://www.universitiesuk.ac.uk/policy-and-analysis/reports/Documents/2018/guidance-for-universities-on-preventing-student-suicides.pdf

240 Ibid.

241 Moffitt, T., and Piquero, A. 'Moffitt's Developmental Taxonomy of Antisocial Behaviour', Encyclopedia of Criminology and Criminal Justice, 27 Nov 2018.

242 Sylvester, R. "The School where you're allowed to hit the teacher', 8 Dec 2018, at https://www.thetimes.co.uk/article/inside-the-boxing-academy-saving-london-children-from-gang-violence-and-knife-crime-m76t2852h

243 This project aims to turn schoolchildren in Europe aged 10-15 into powerful lie detectors and critical thinkers in a world increasingly populated by propaganda and distorted facts online, empowering them to understand news media, make informed choices and resist peer pressure as they assemble their worldview. See www.lie-detectors.org

244 Department for Education, 'Elective Home Education: Departmental Guidance for Parents', April 2019, at https://assets.publishing.service.gov.uk/government/uploads/system/uploads/attachment_data/file/791528/EHE_guidance_for_parentsafter-consultationv2.2.pdf

245 Department for Education, 'Report of the Independent Panel on Technical Education', April 2016, at https://assets.publishing.service.gov.uk/government/uploads/system/uploads/attachment_data/file/536046/Report_of_the_Independent_Panel_on_Technical_Education.pdf (and see reference to 13,000 qualifications available to 16-18 year olds).

246 Department for Education, 'National curriculum in England: history programmes of study', 11 Sept 2013, at https://www.gov.uk/government/publications/national-curriculum-in-england-history-programmes-of-study

247 Rory Smith, 'IQ scores are falling and have been for decades, new study finds', 14 June 2018, at https://edition.cnn.com/2018/06/13/health/falling-iq-scores-study-intl/index.html

248 Varkey Foundation, 'Global teacher status index 2018', at https://www.varkeyfoundation.org/what-we-do/policy-research/global-teacher-status-index-2018/